ADULT COLORING BOOK

NEW ABSTRACT DESIGNS

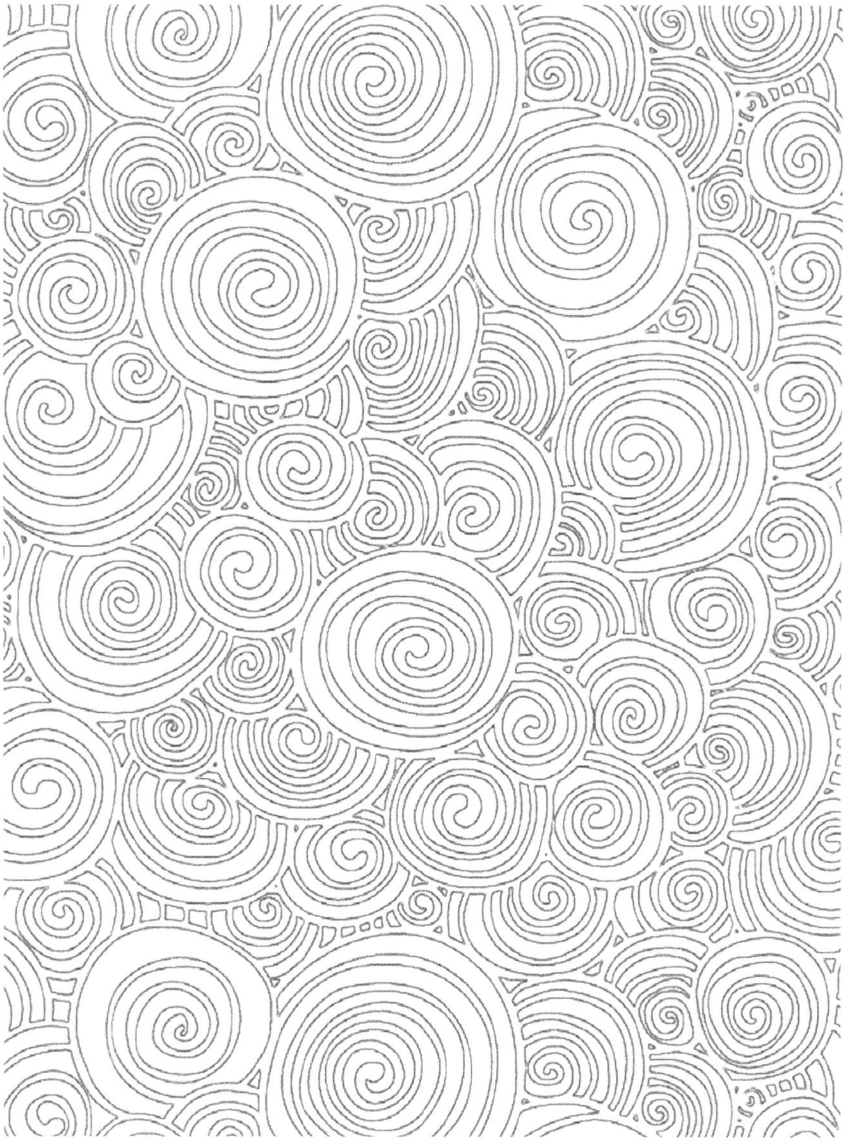

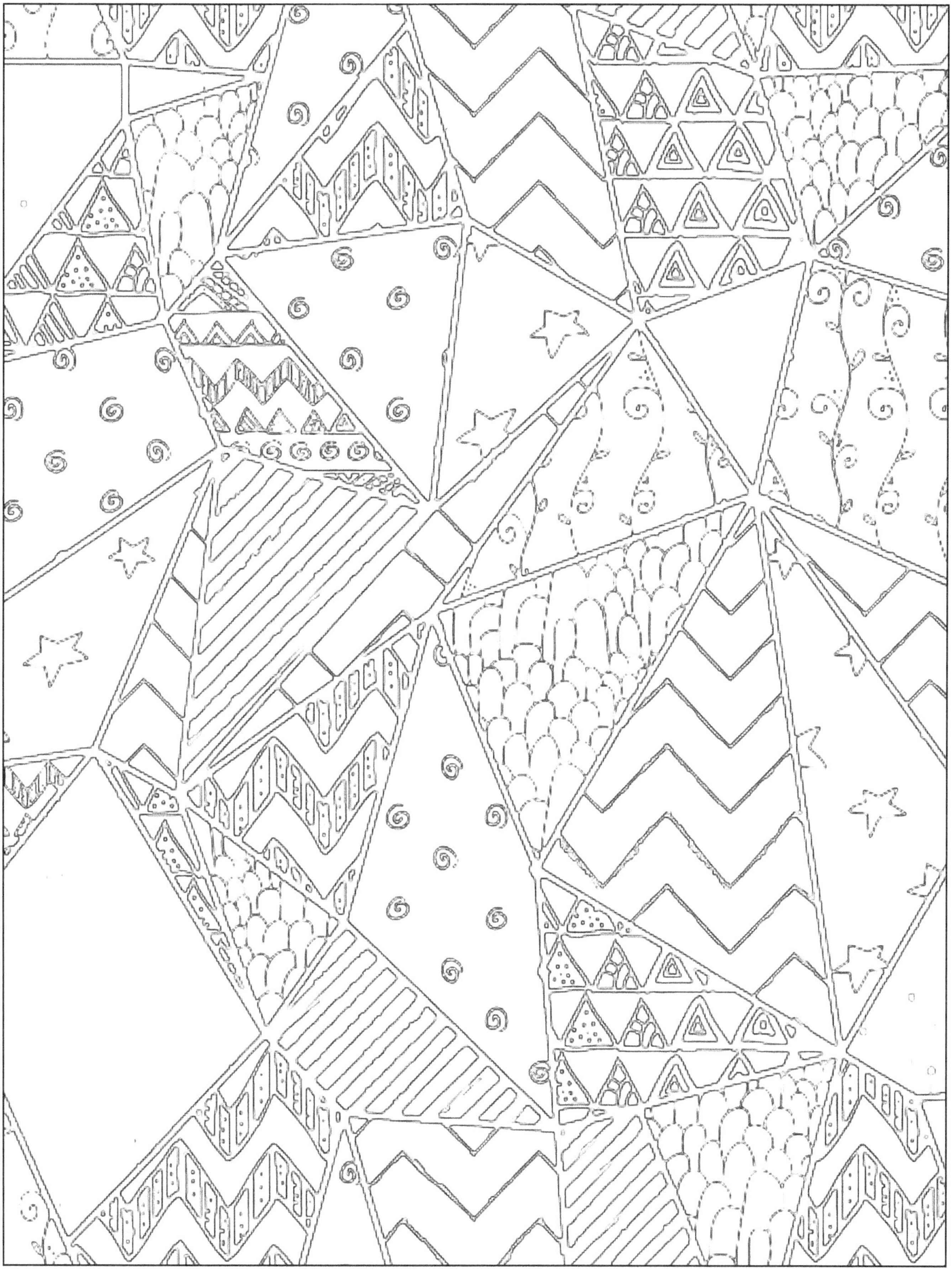

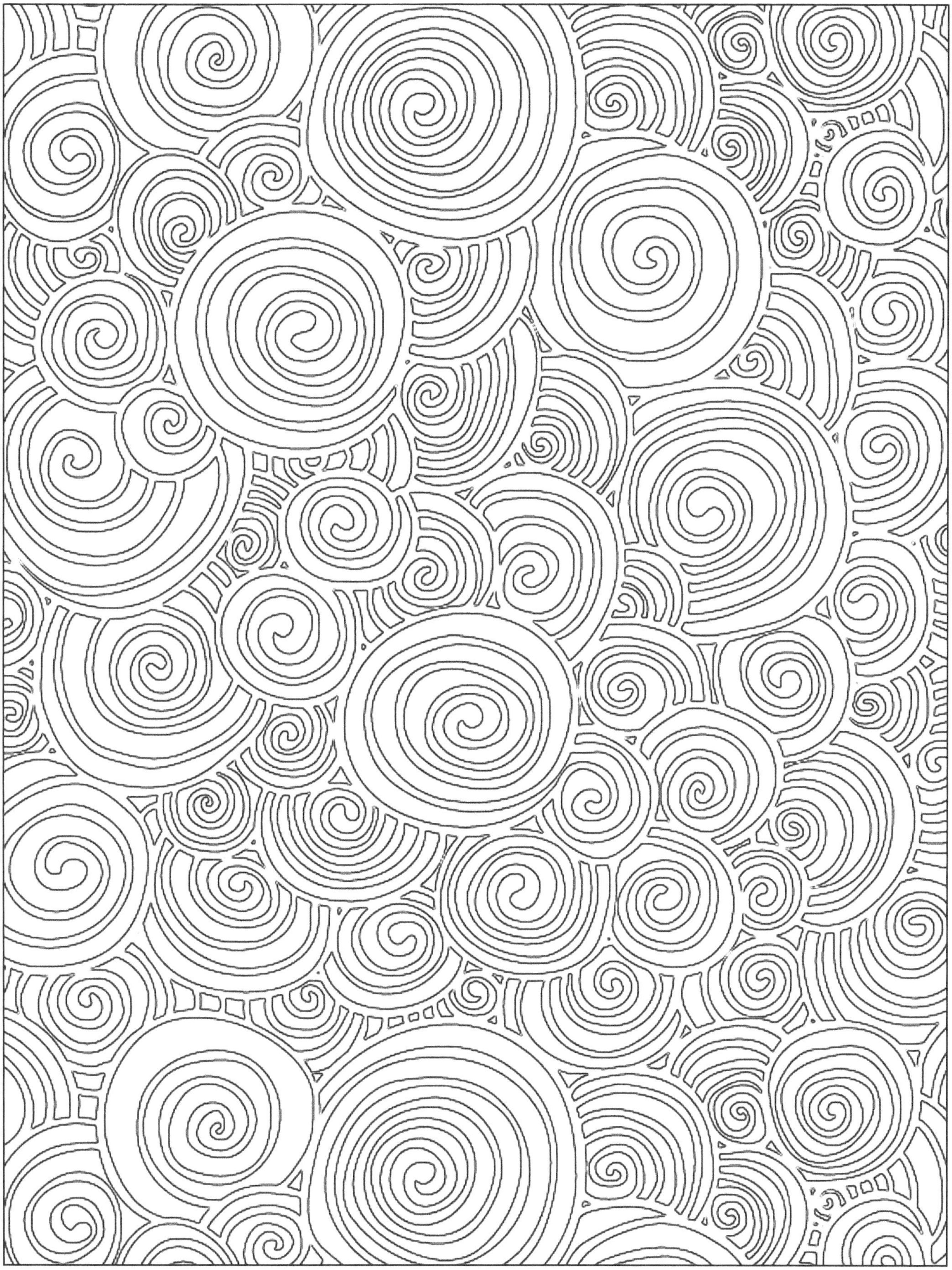

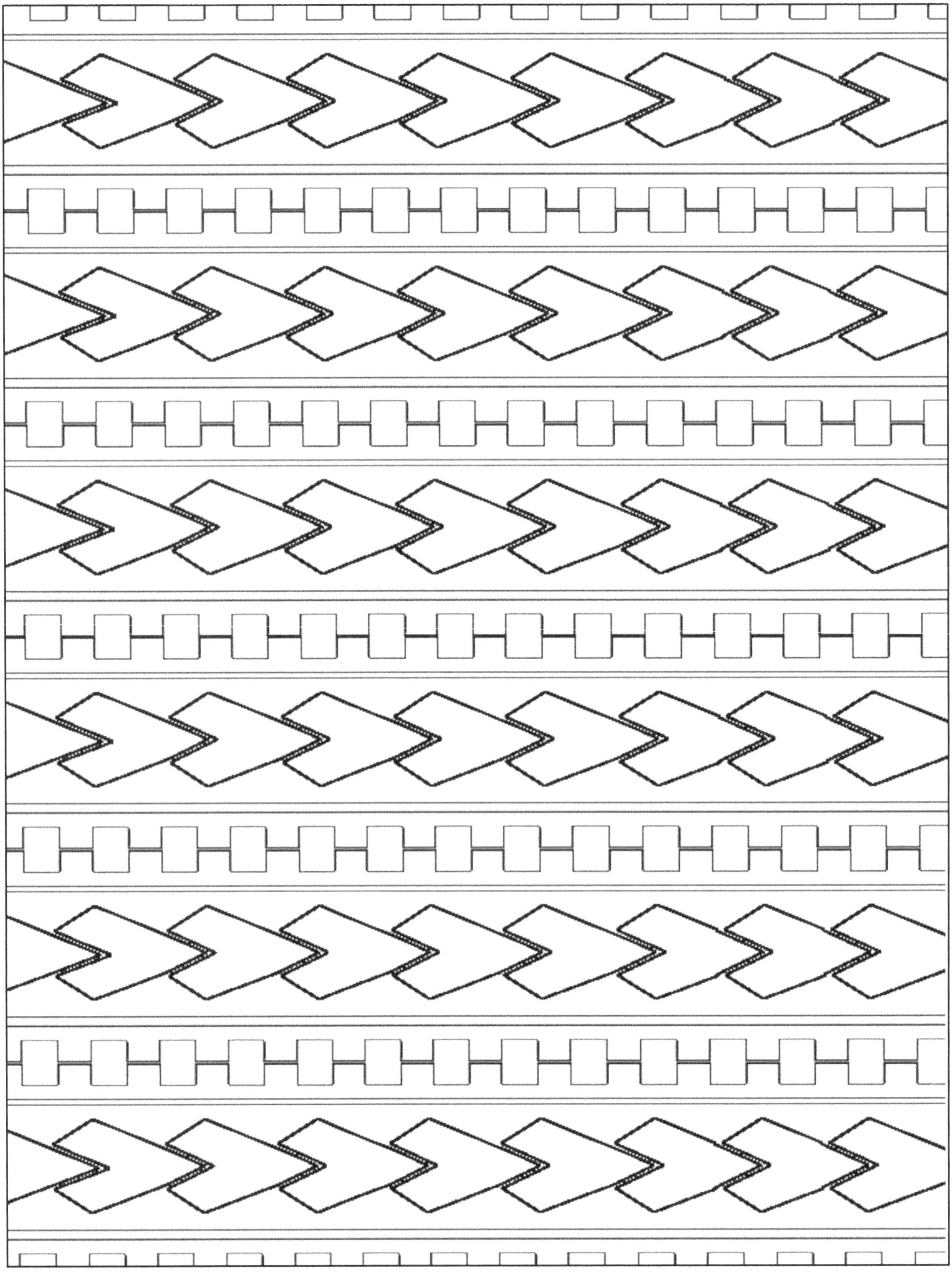

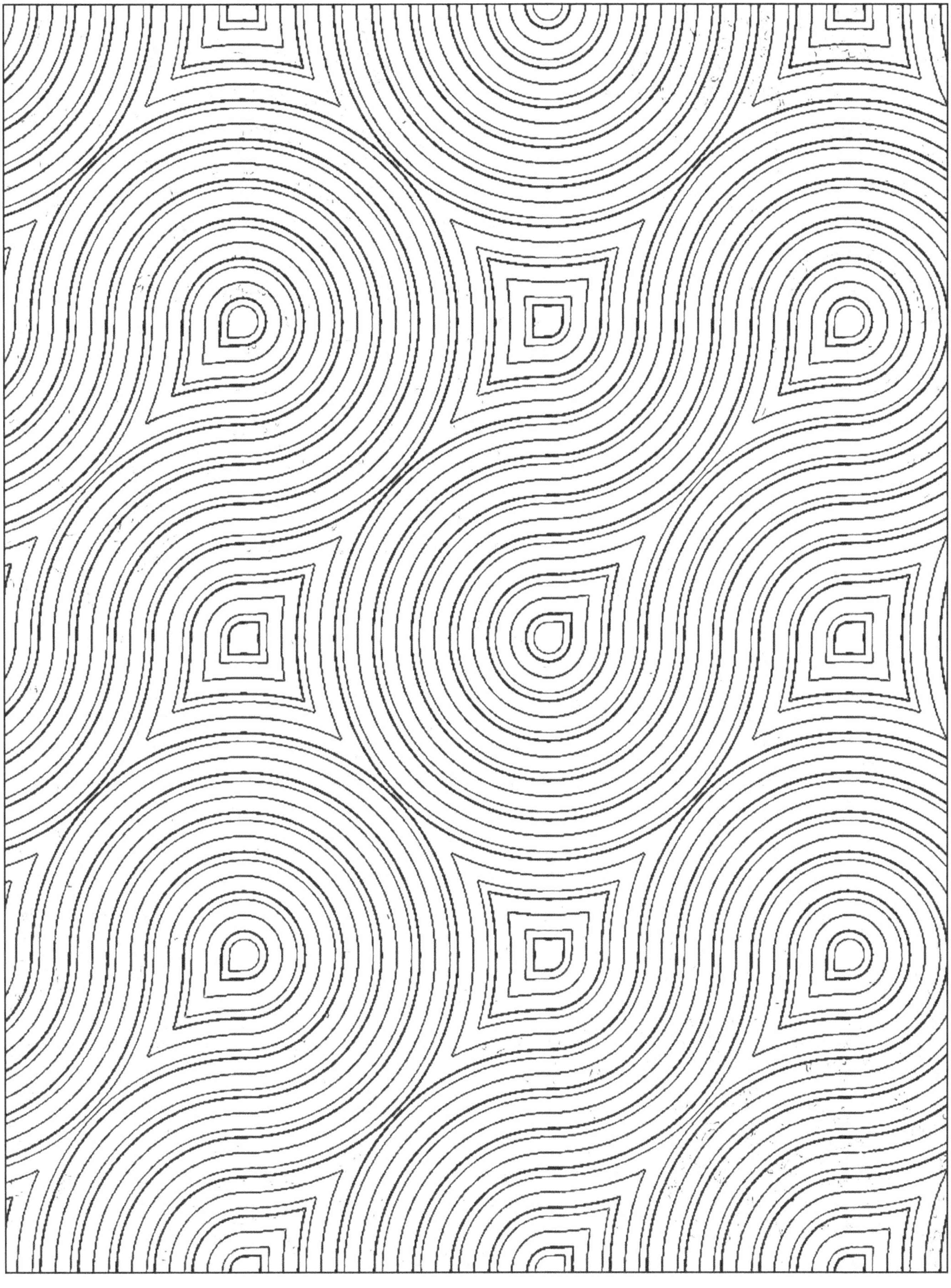

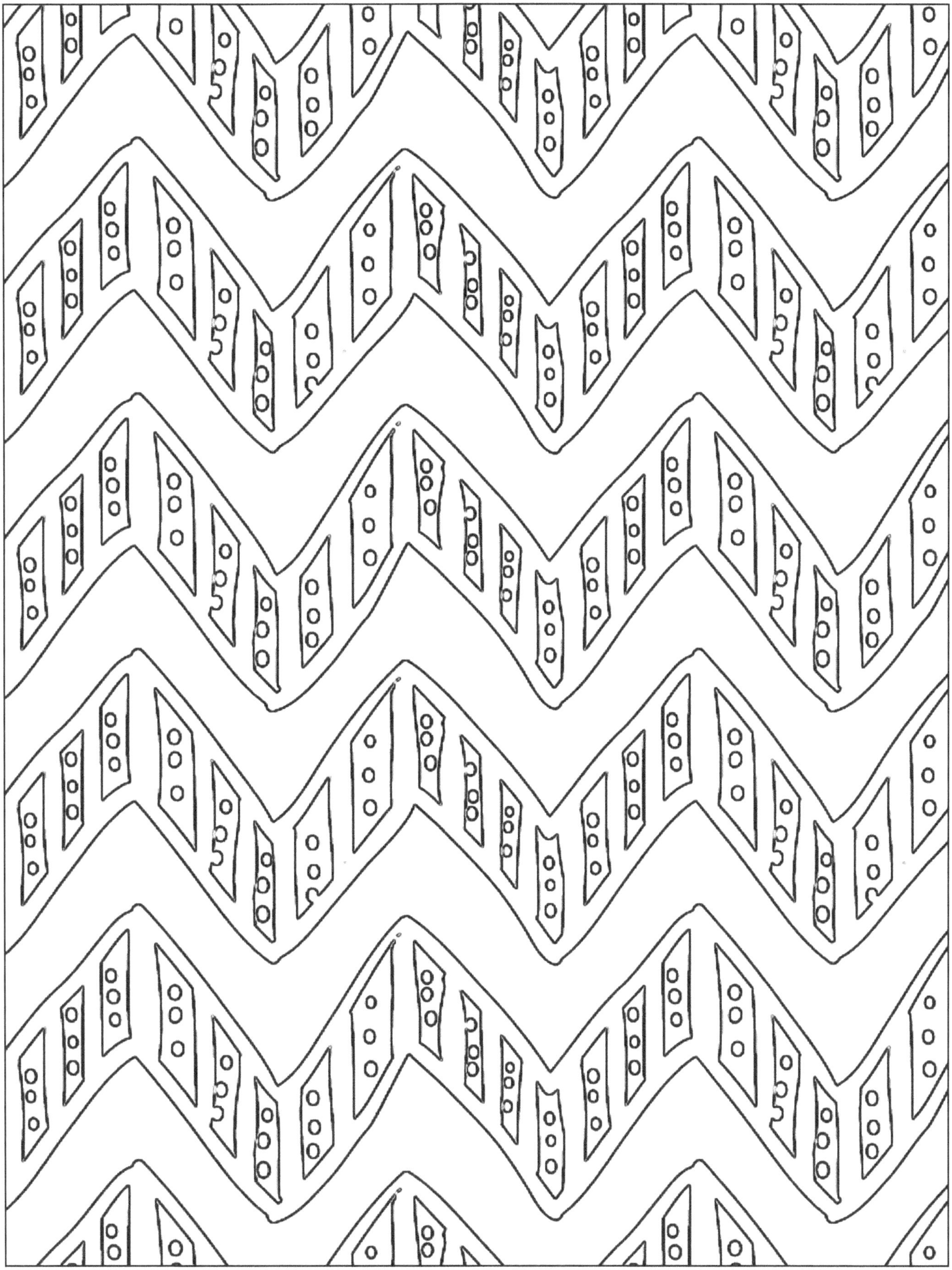

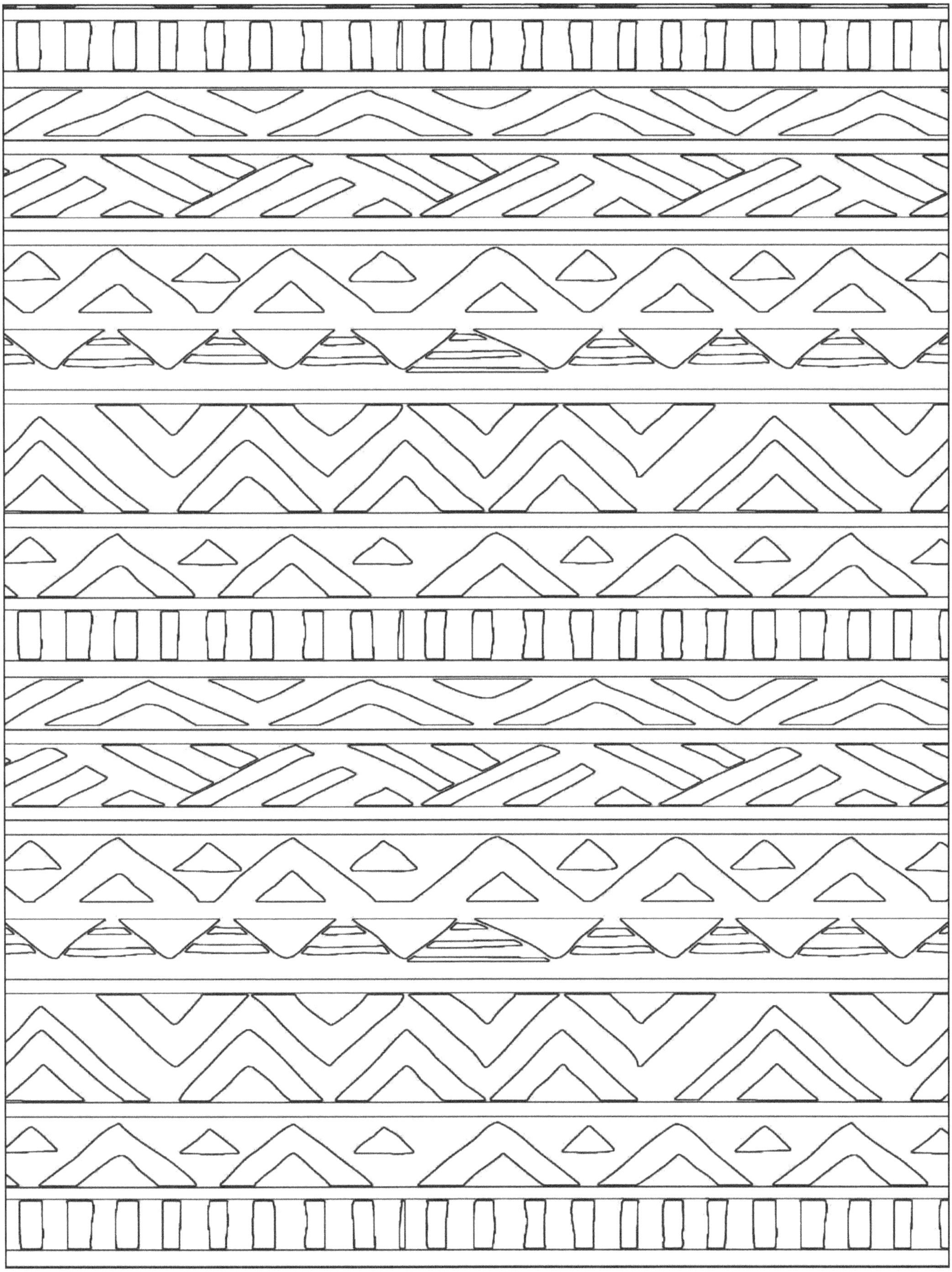

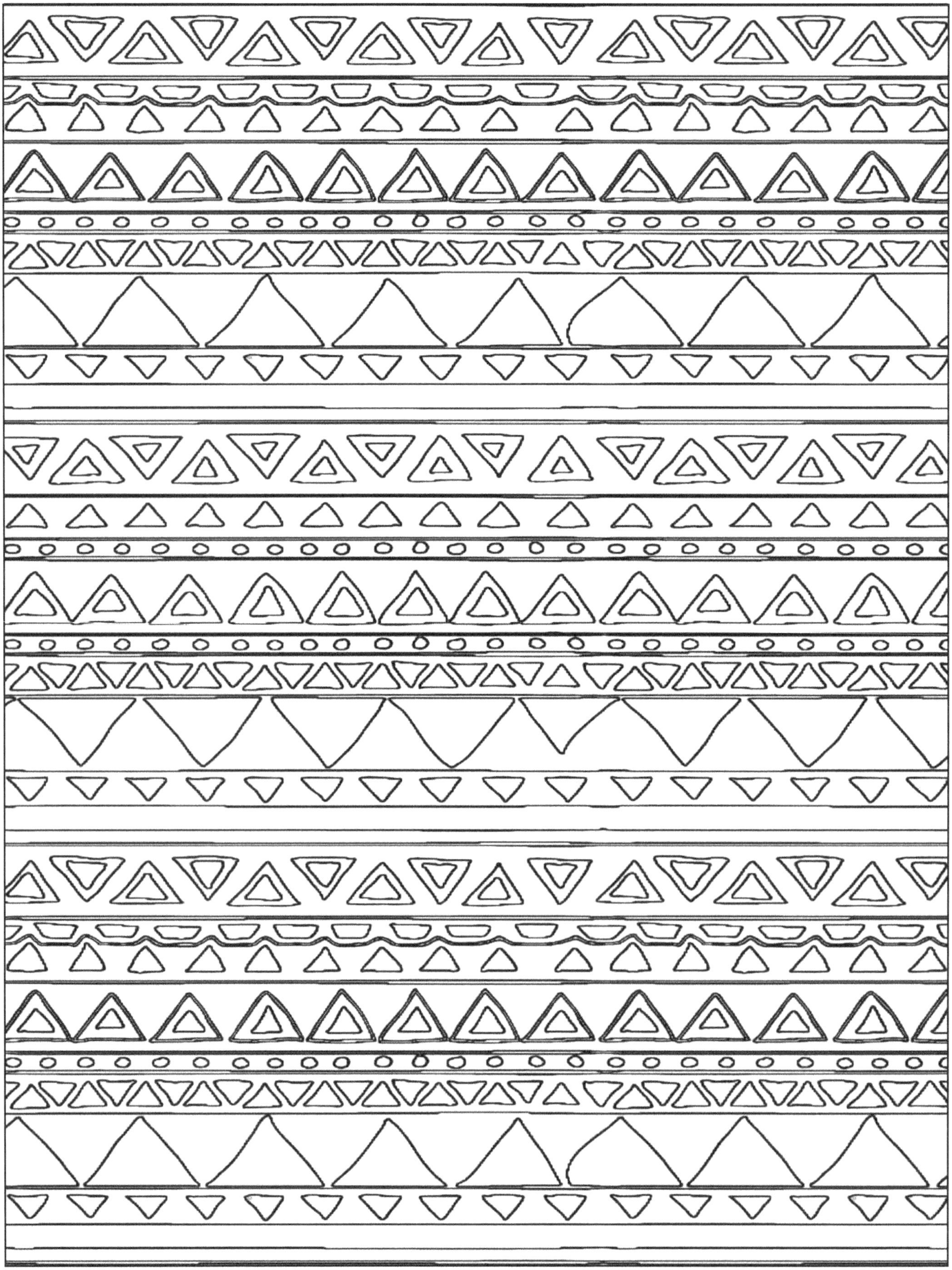

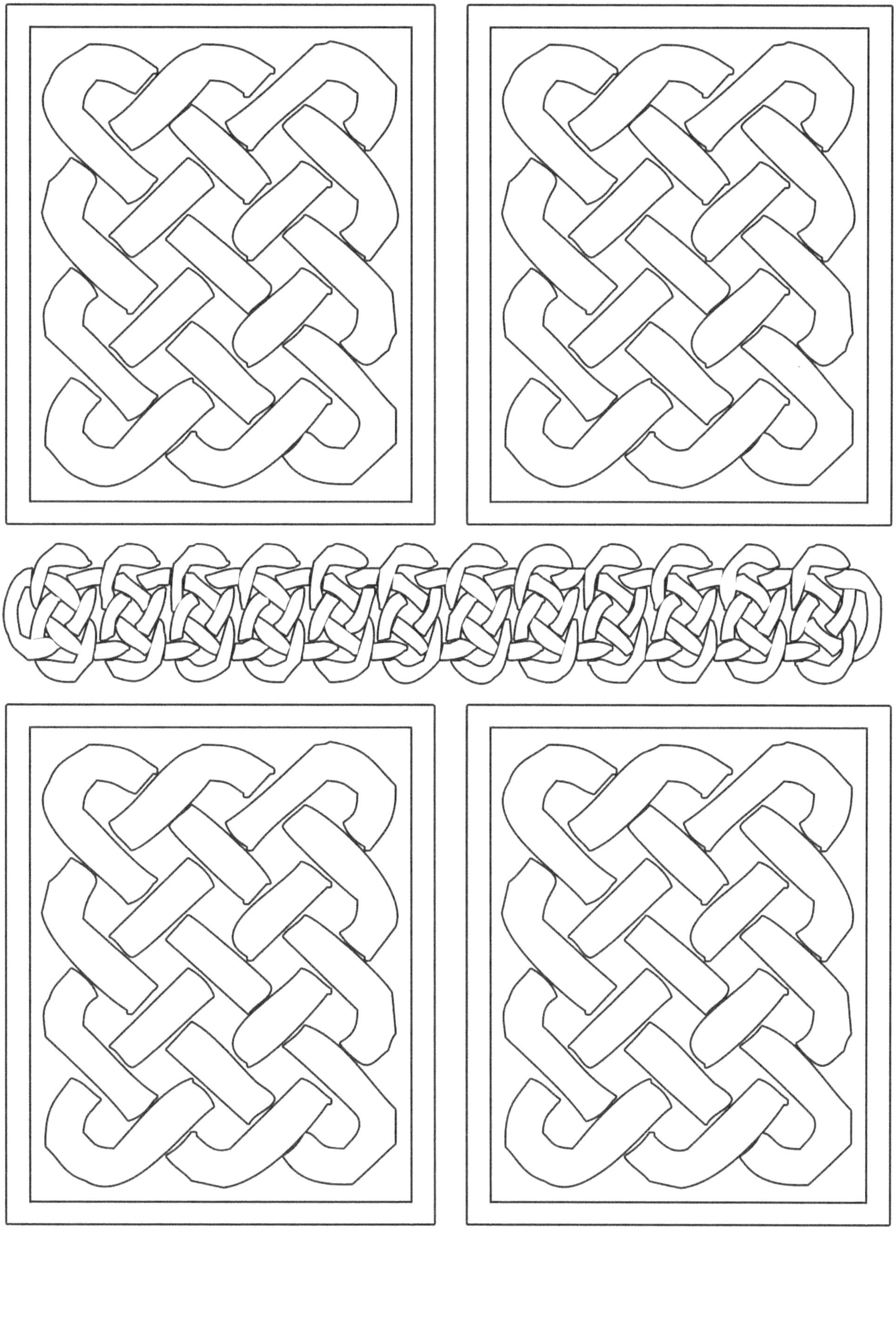

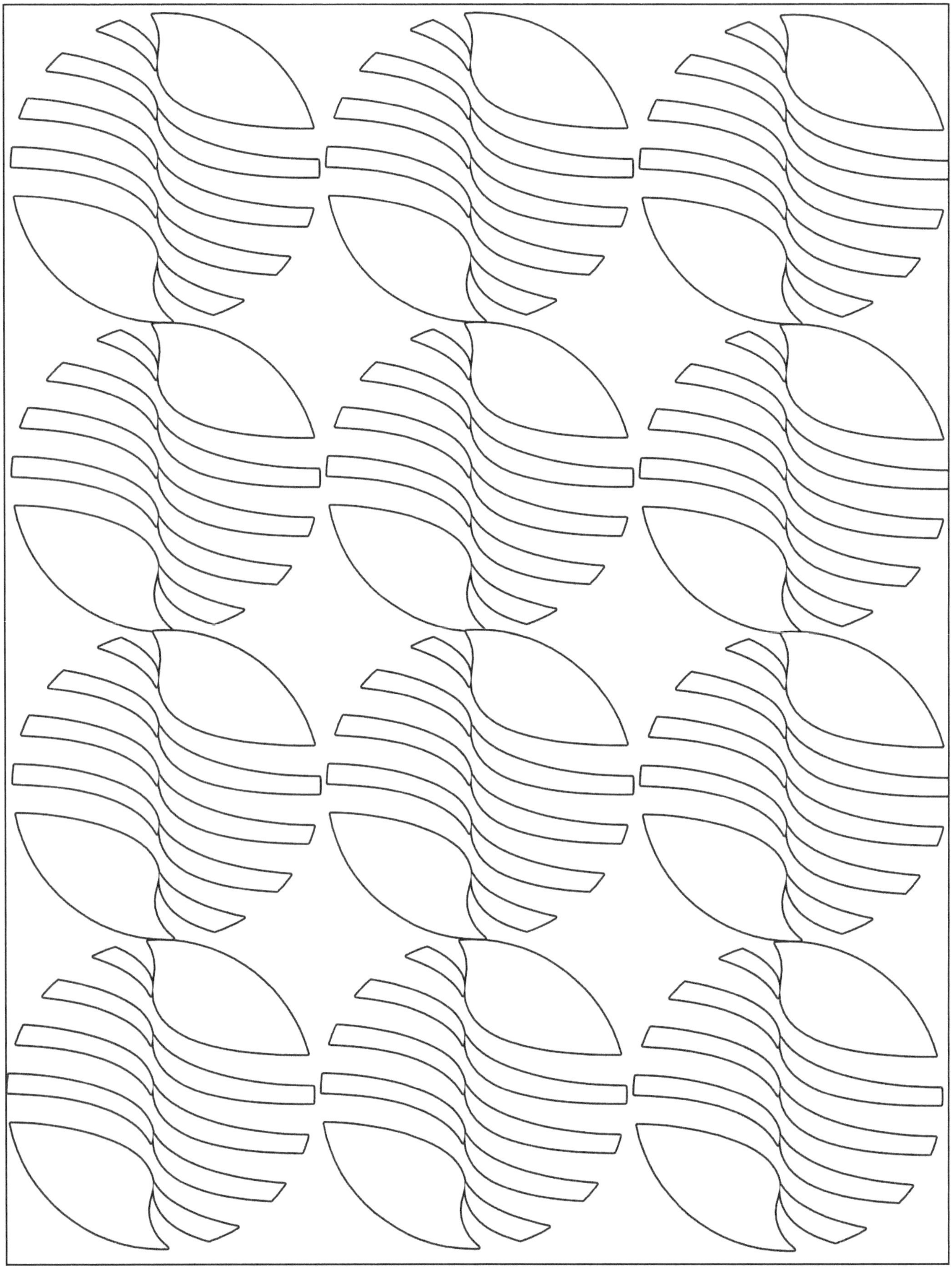

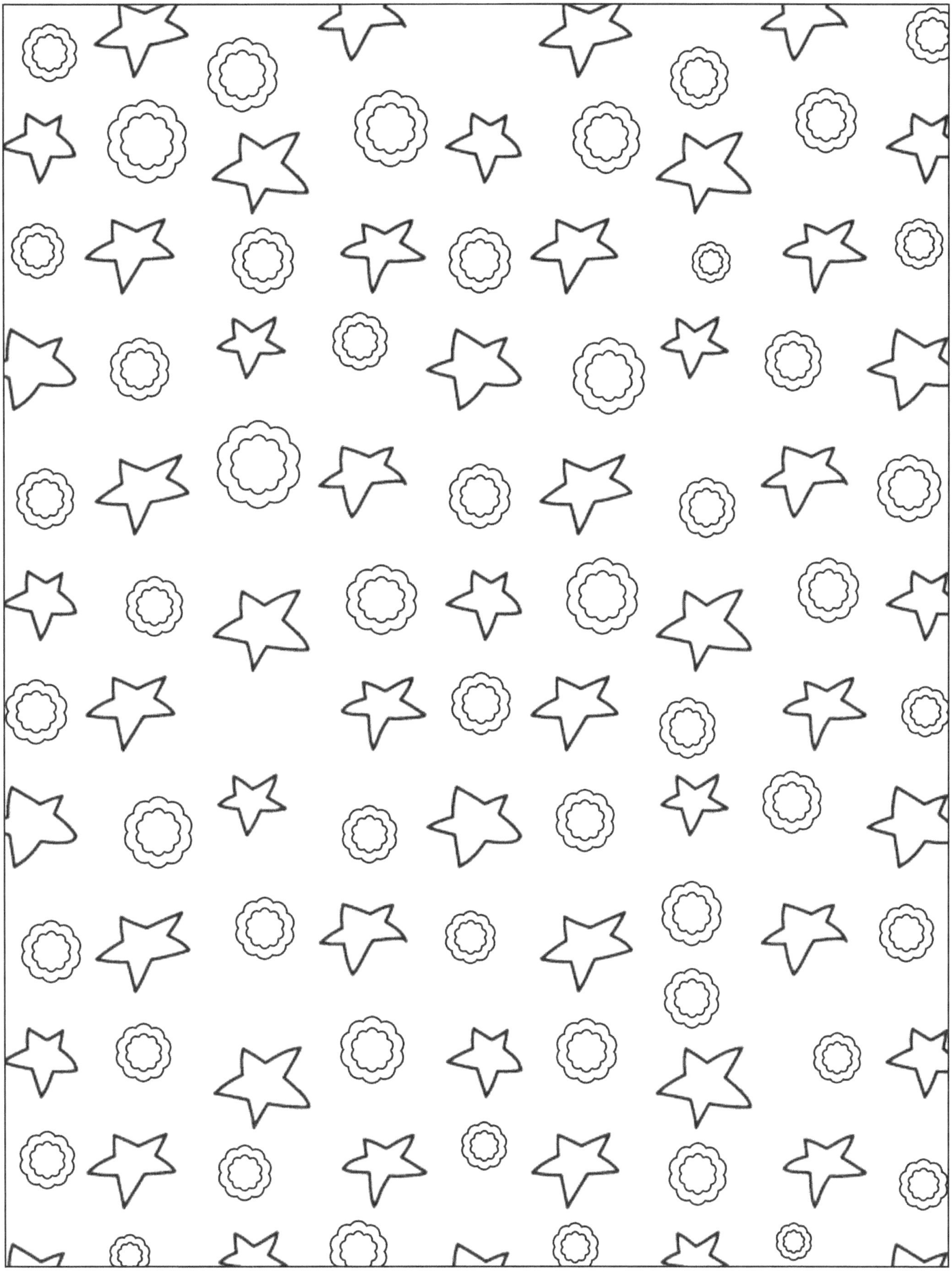

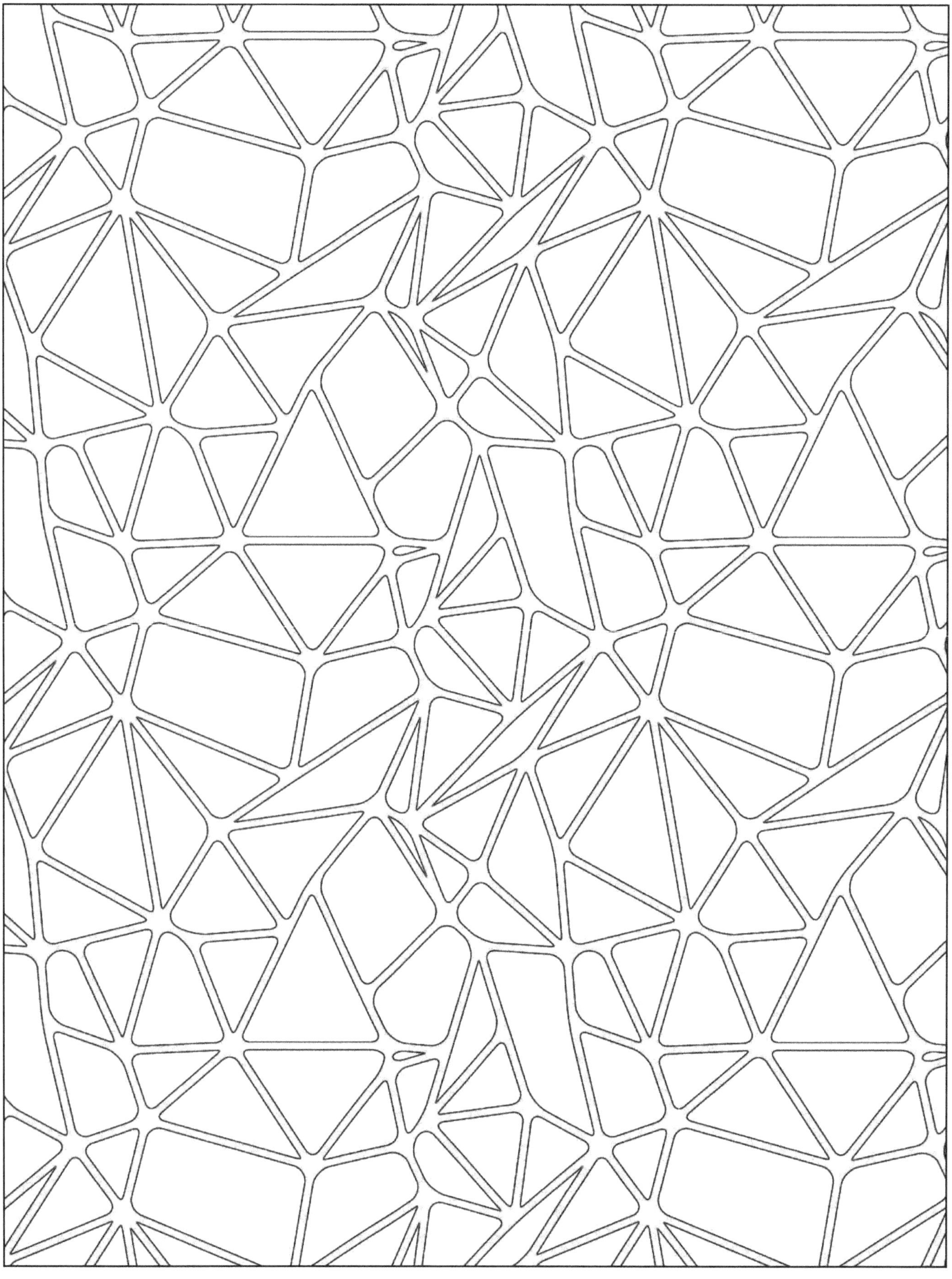

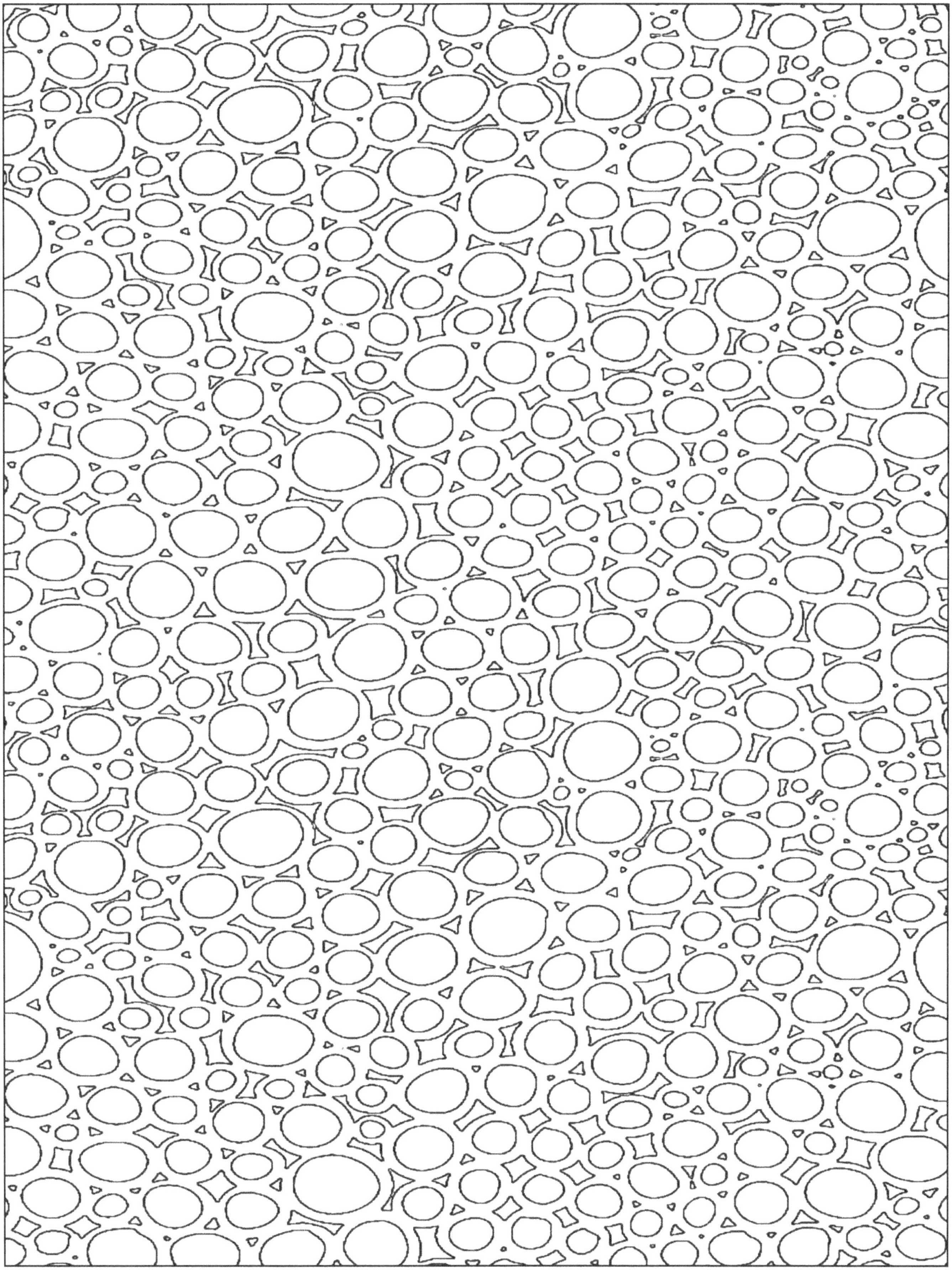

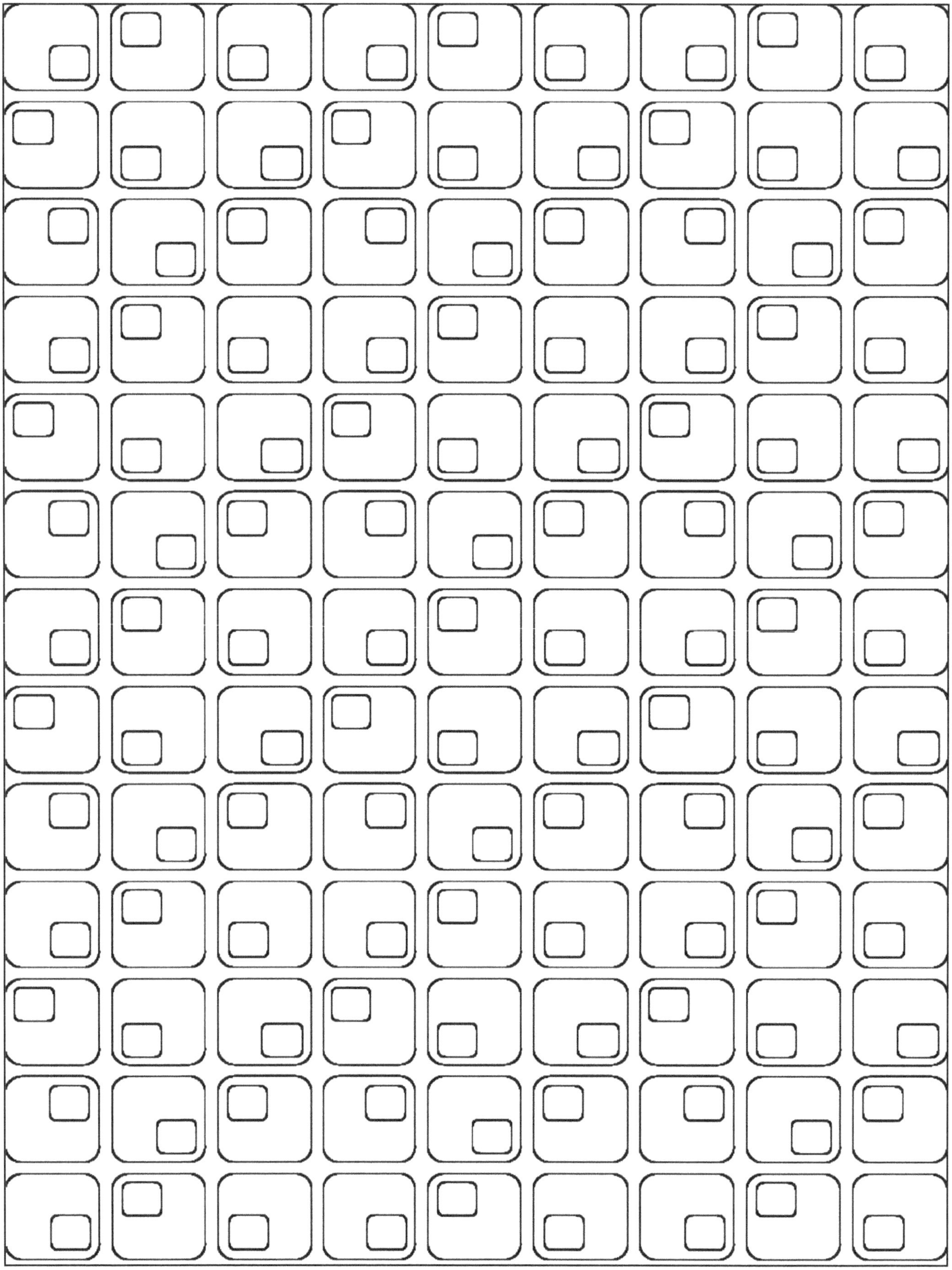

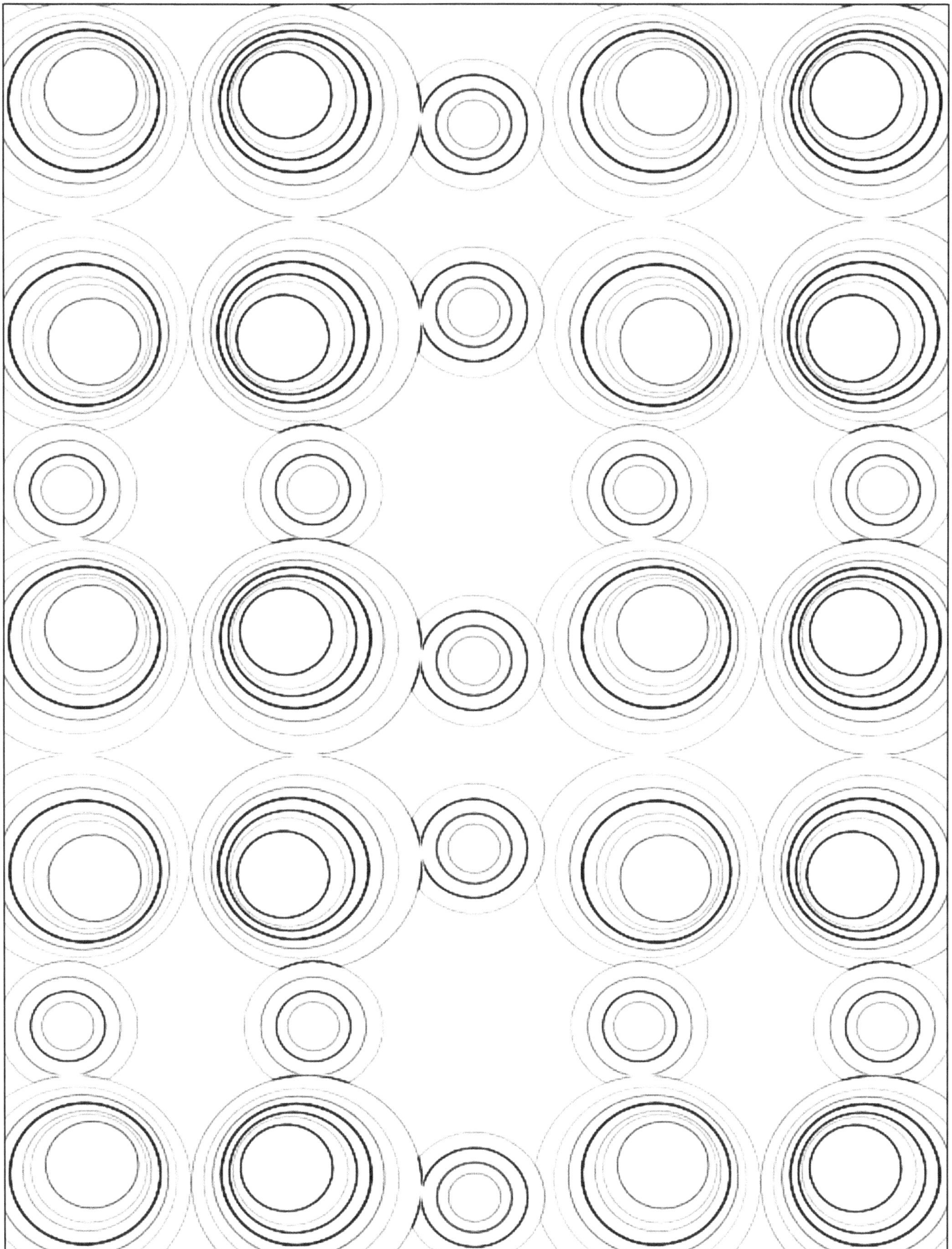

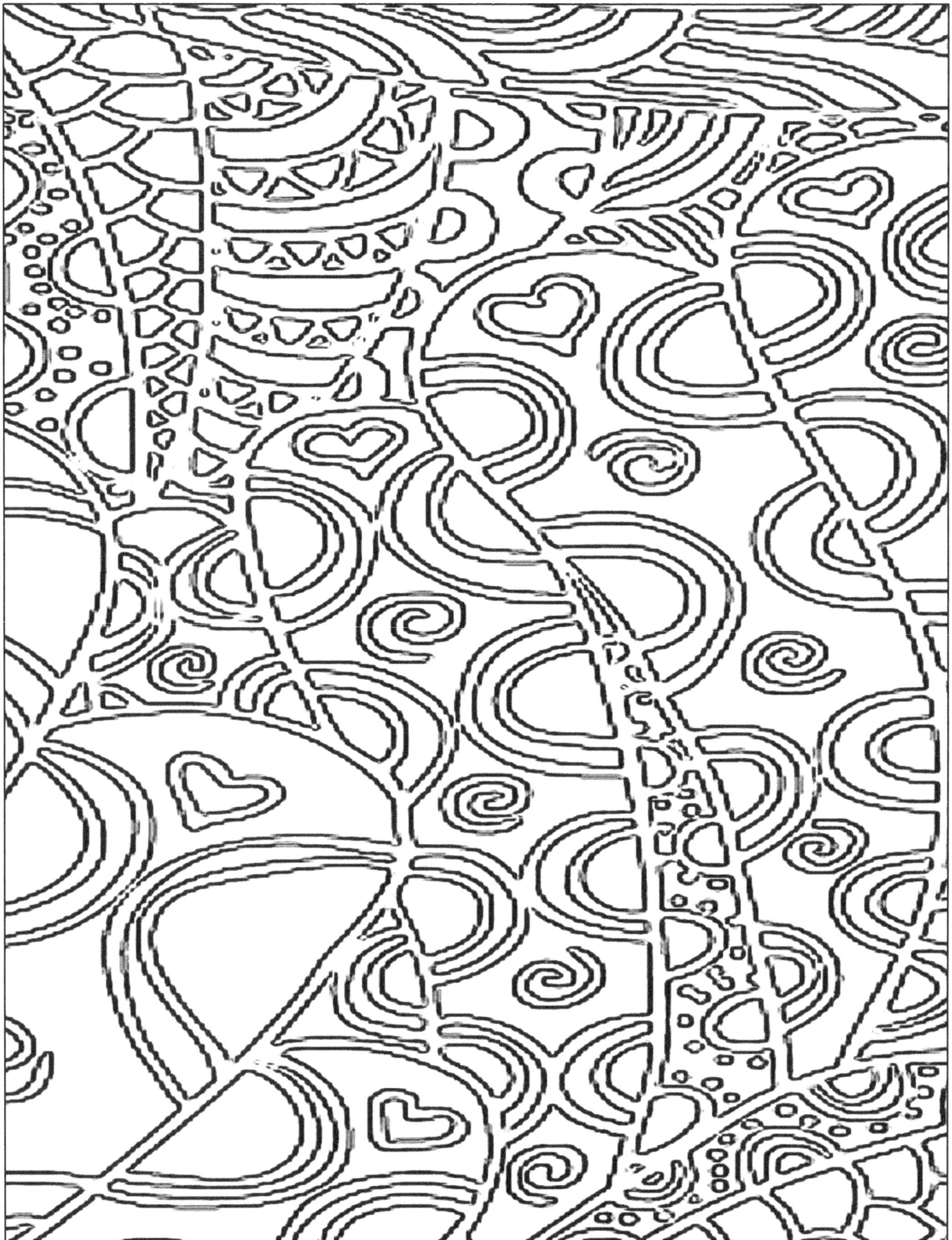

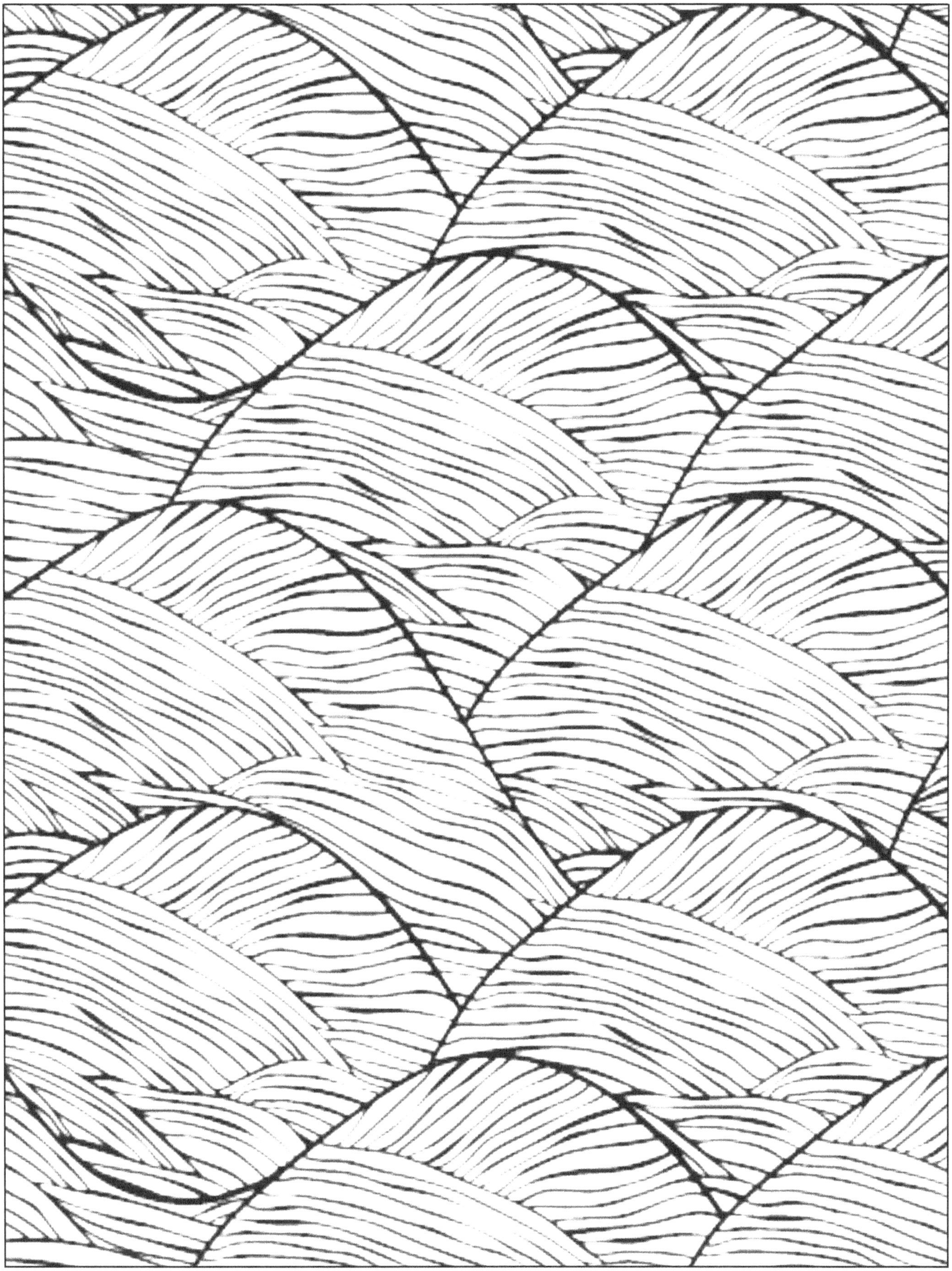

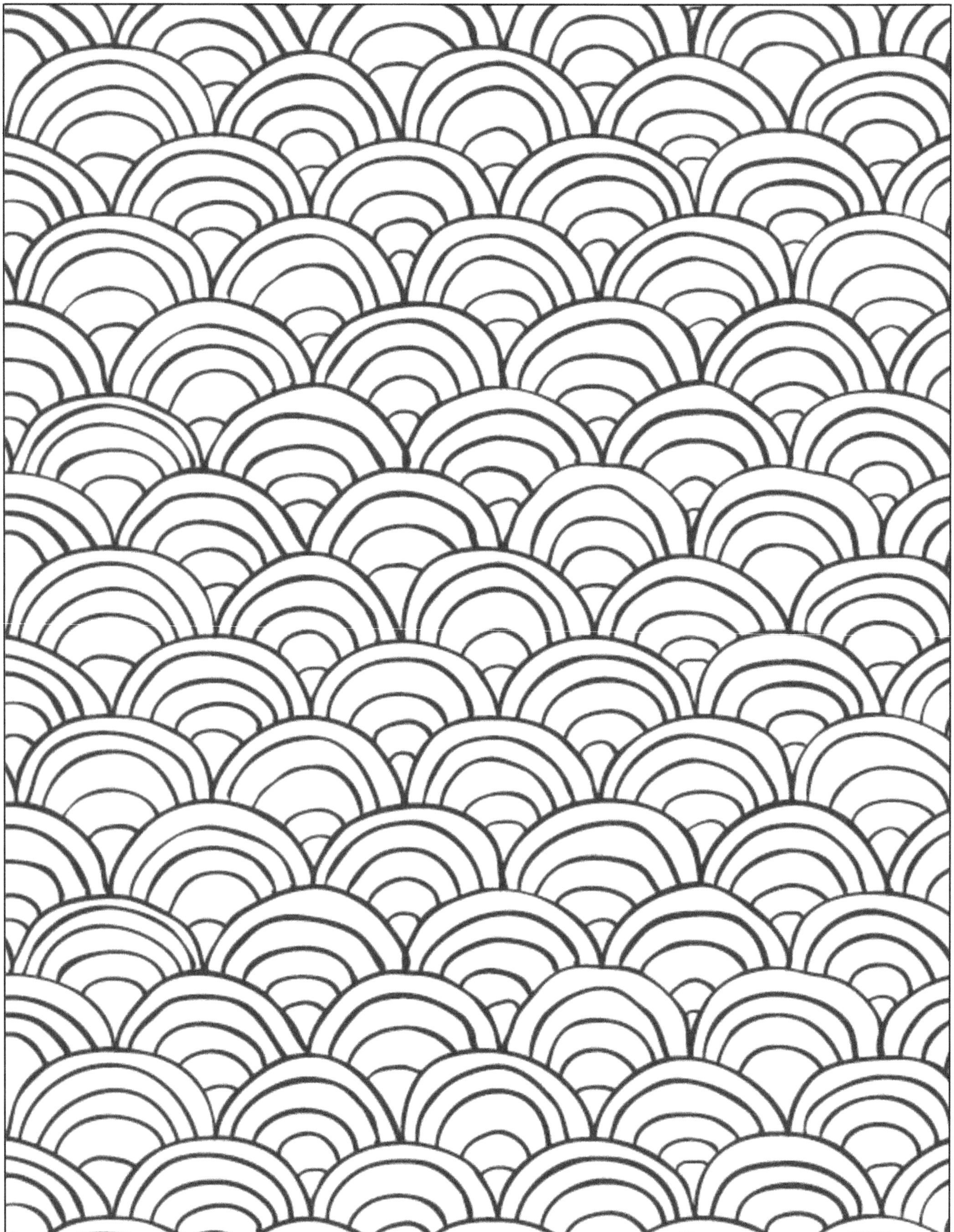

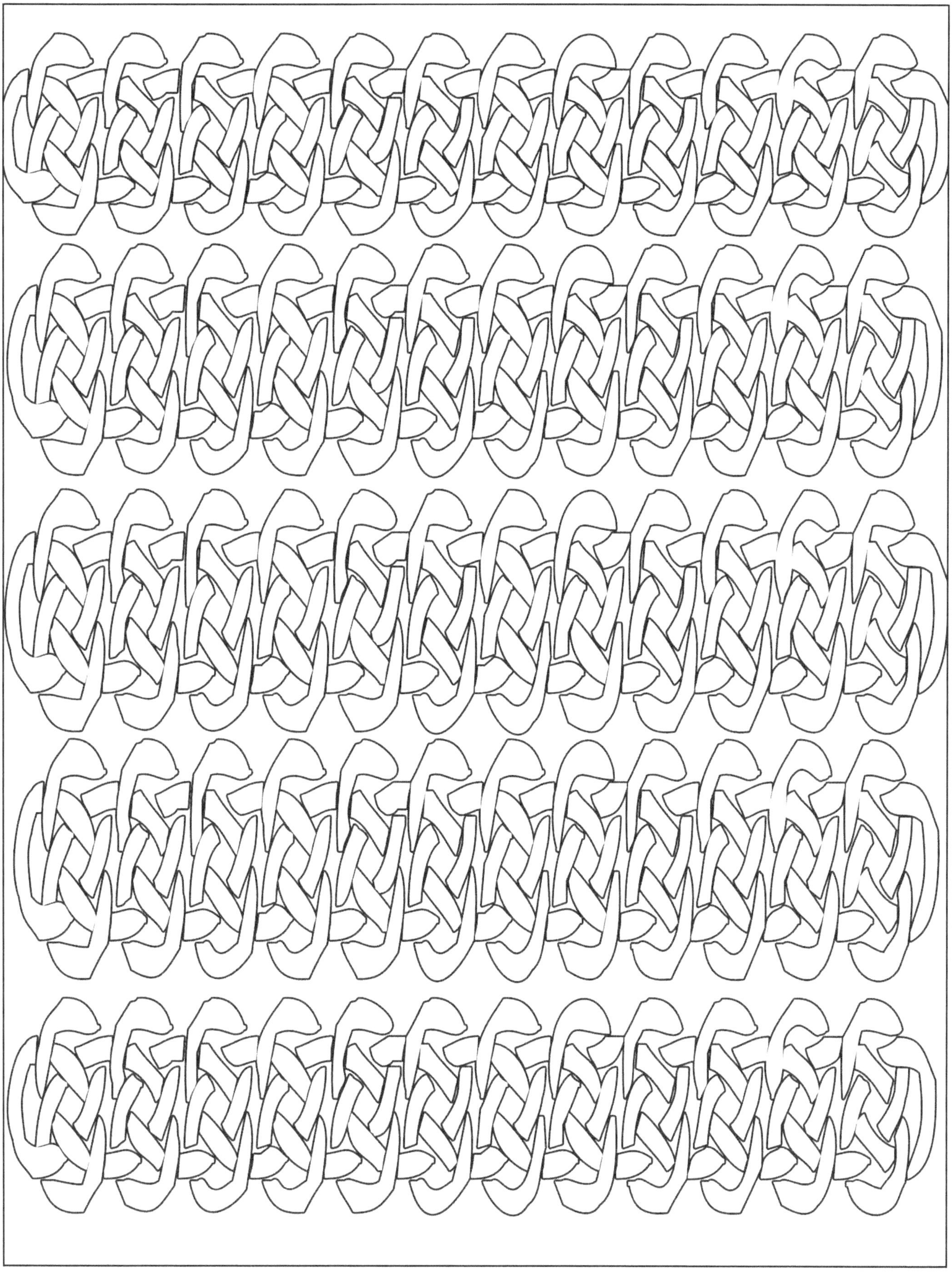

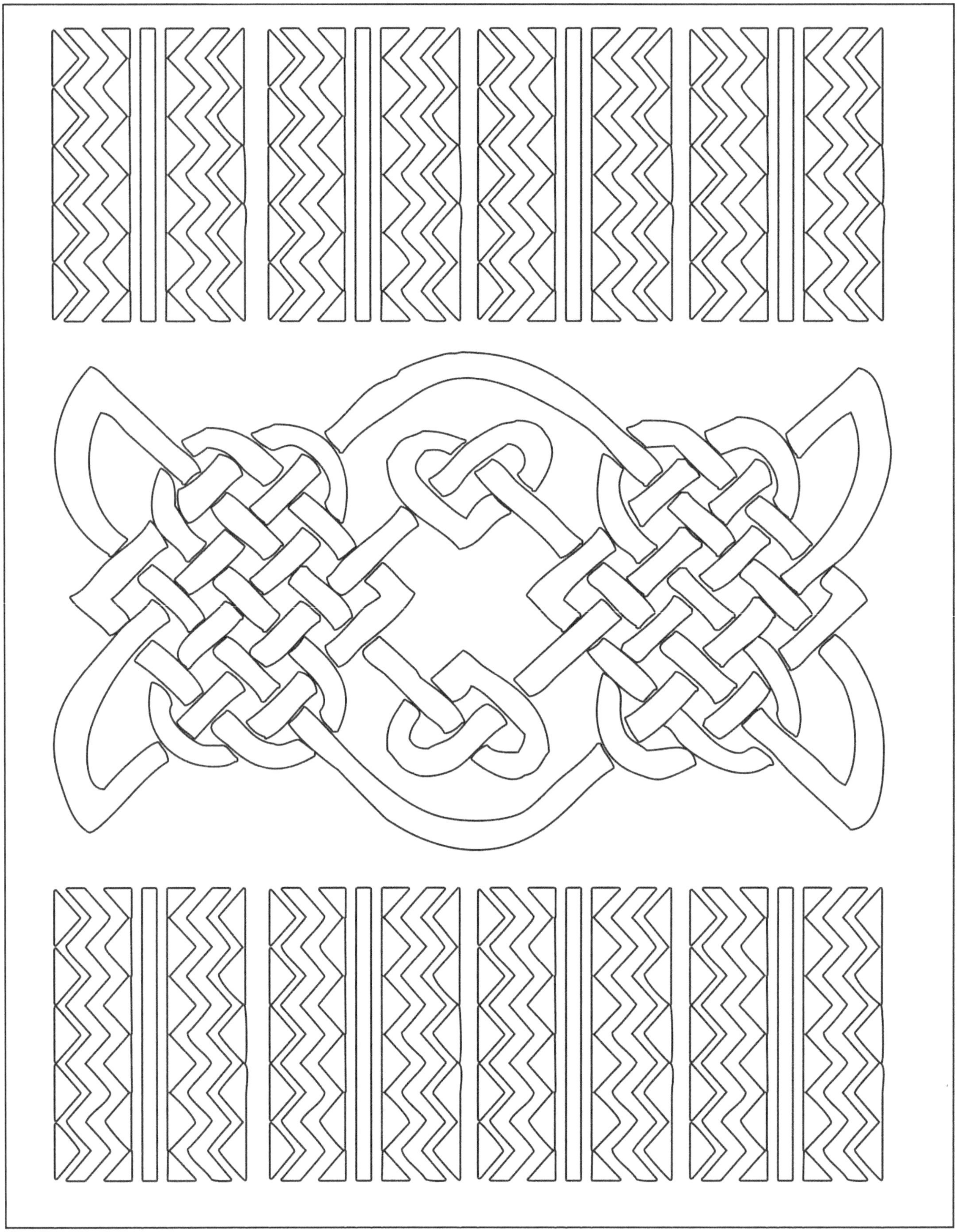

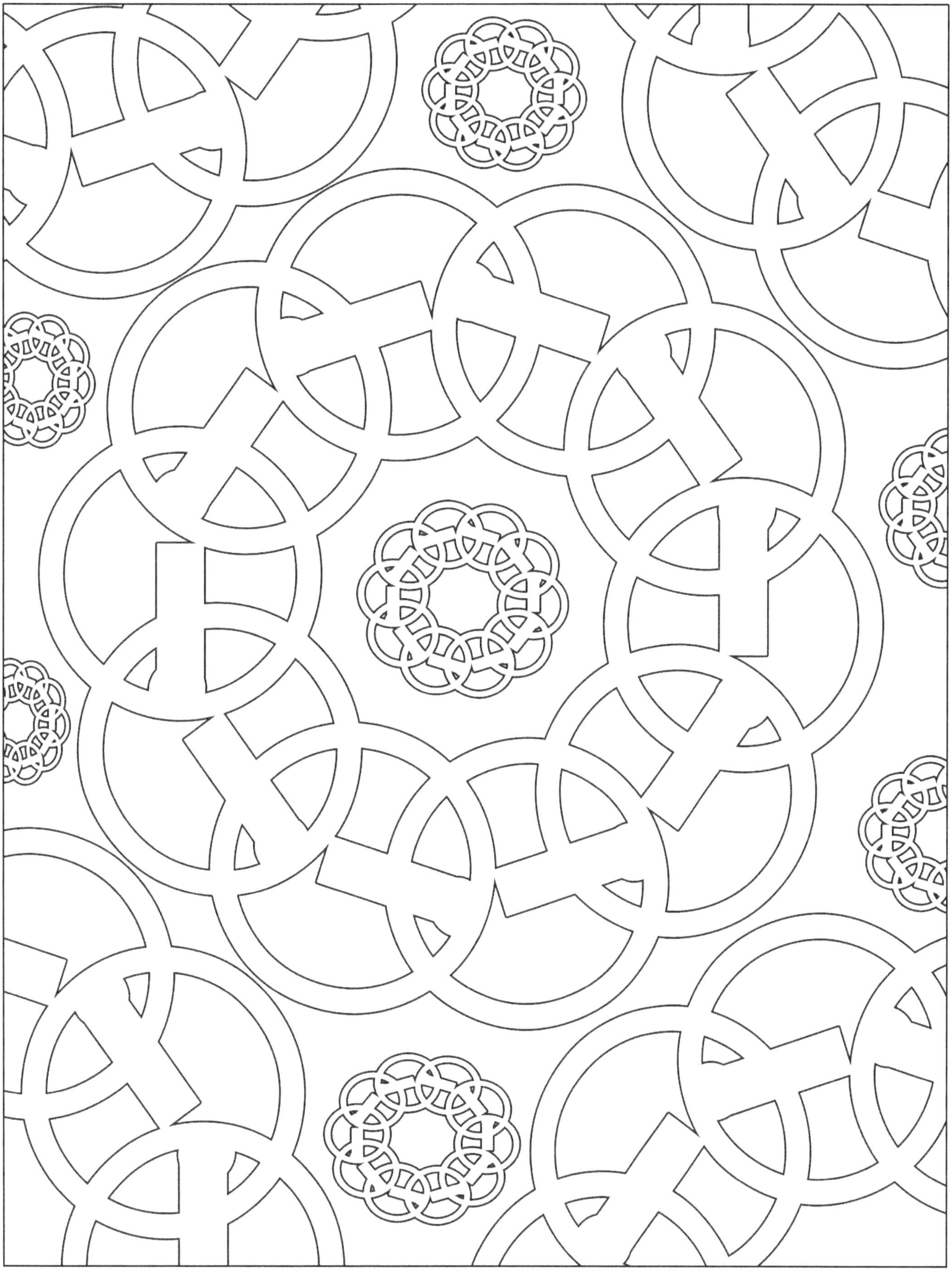

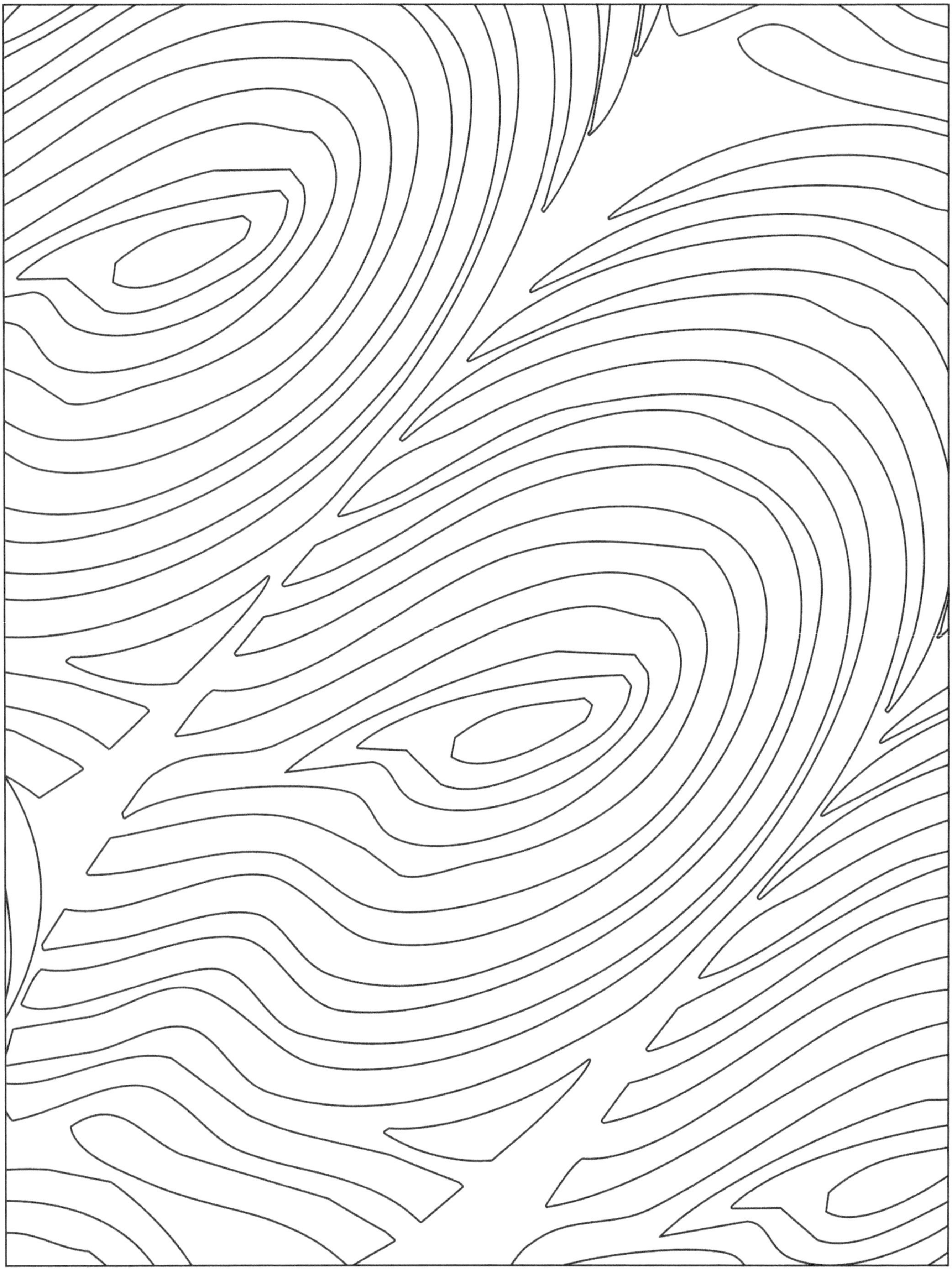

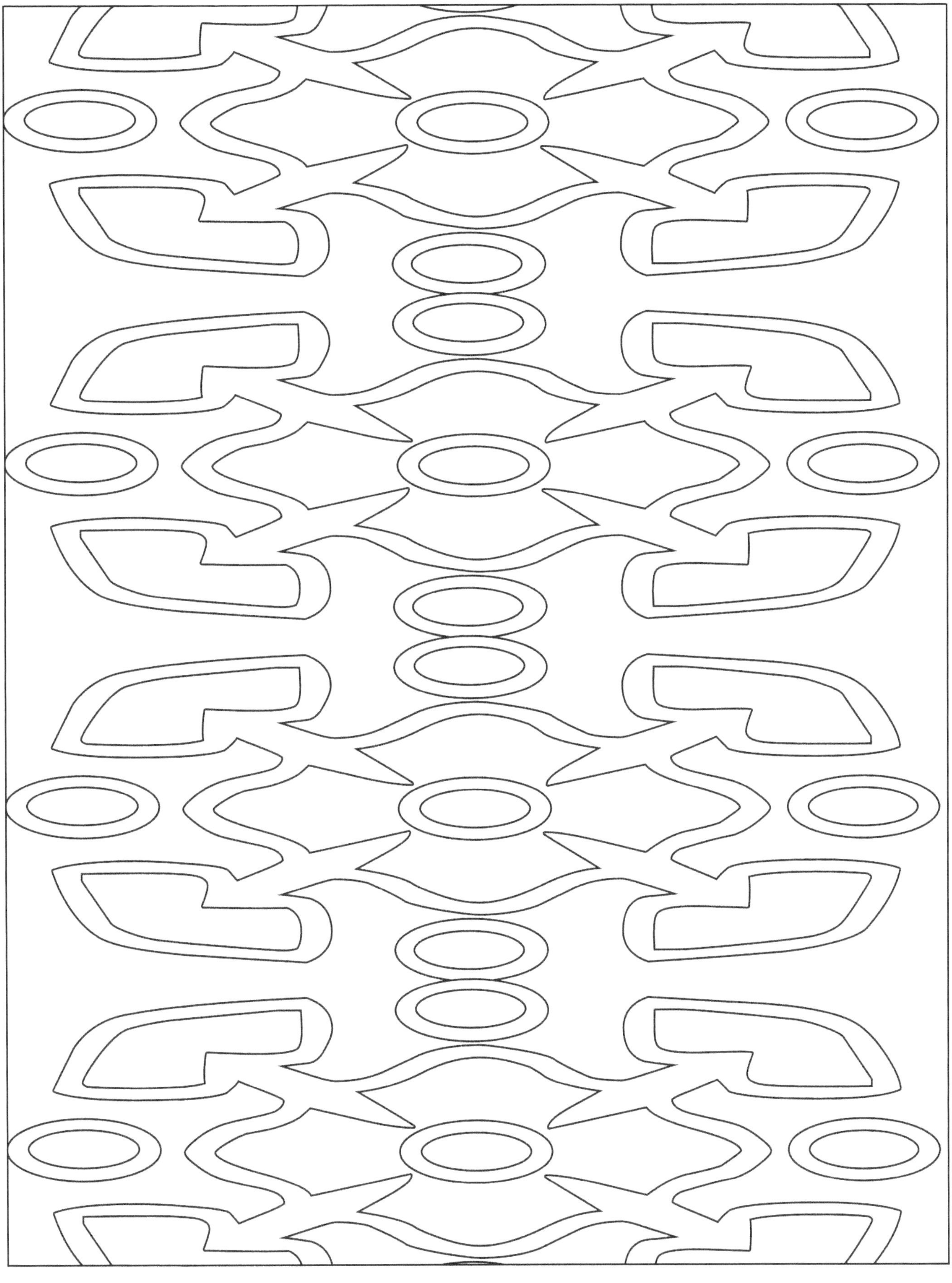

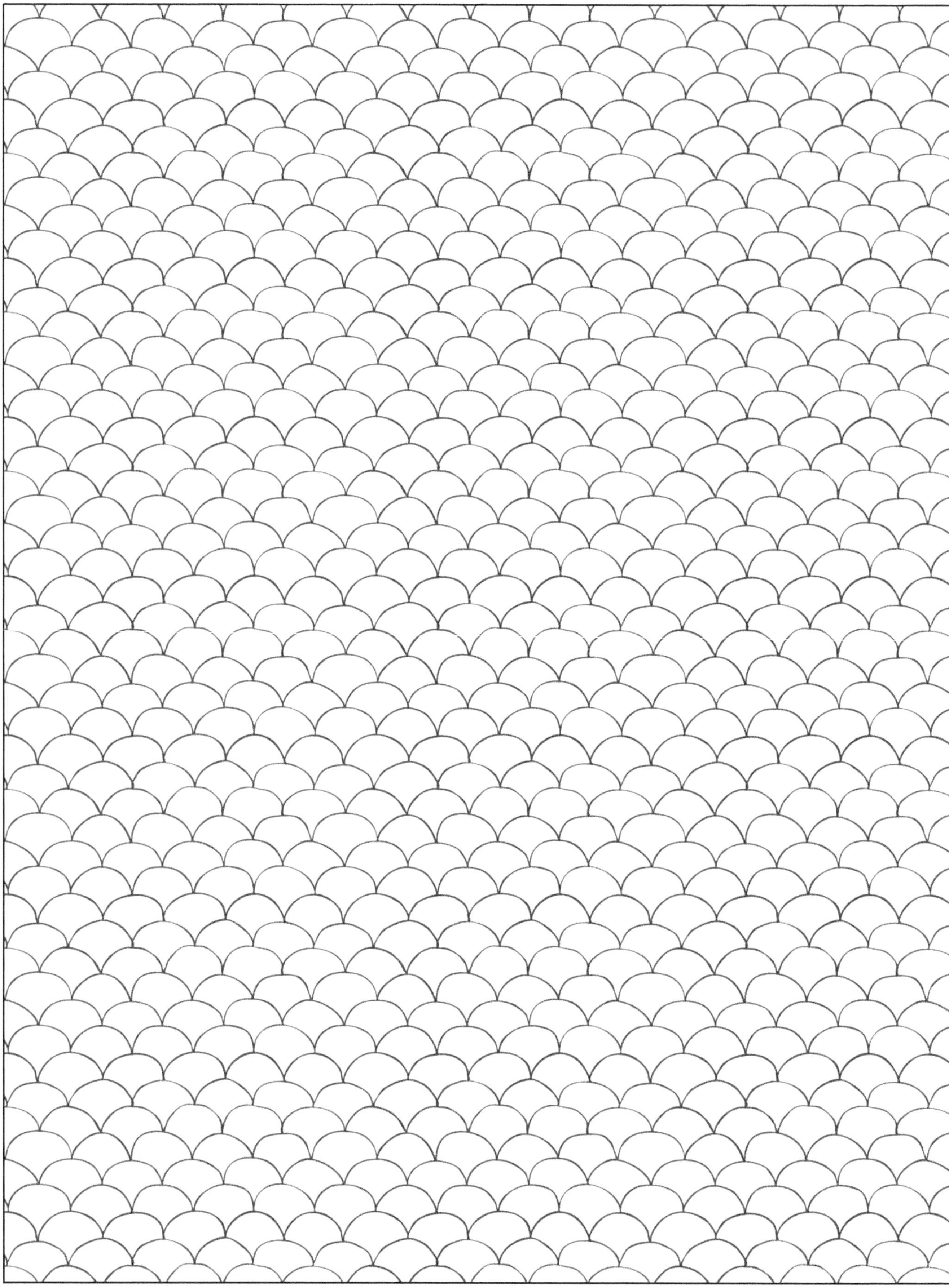

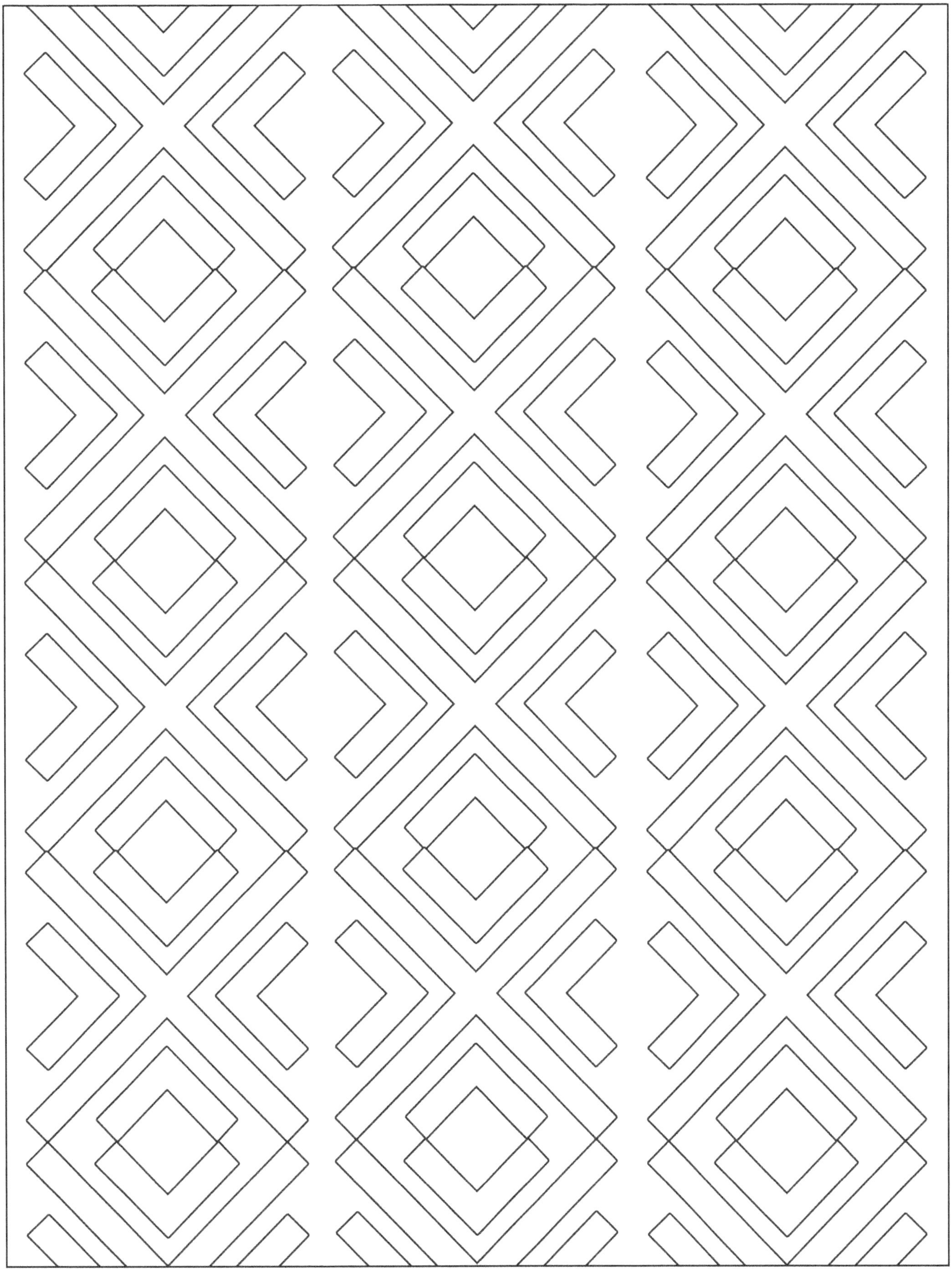

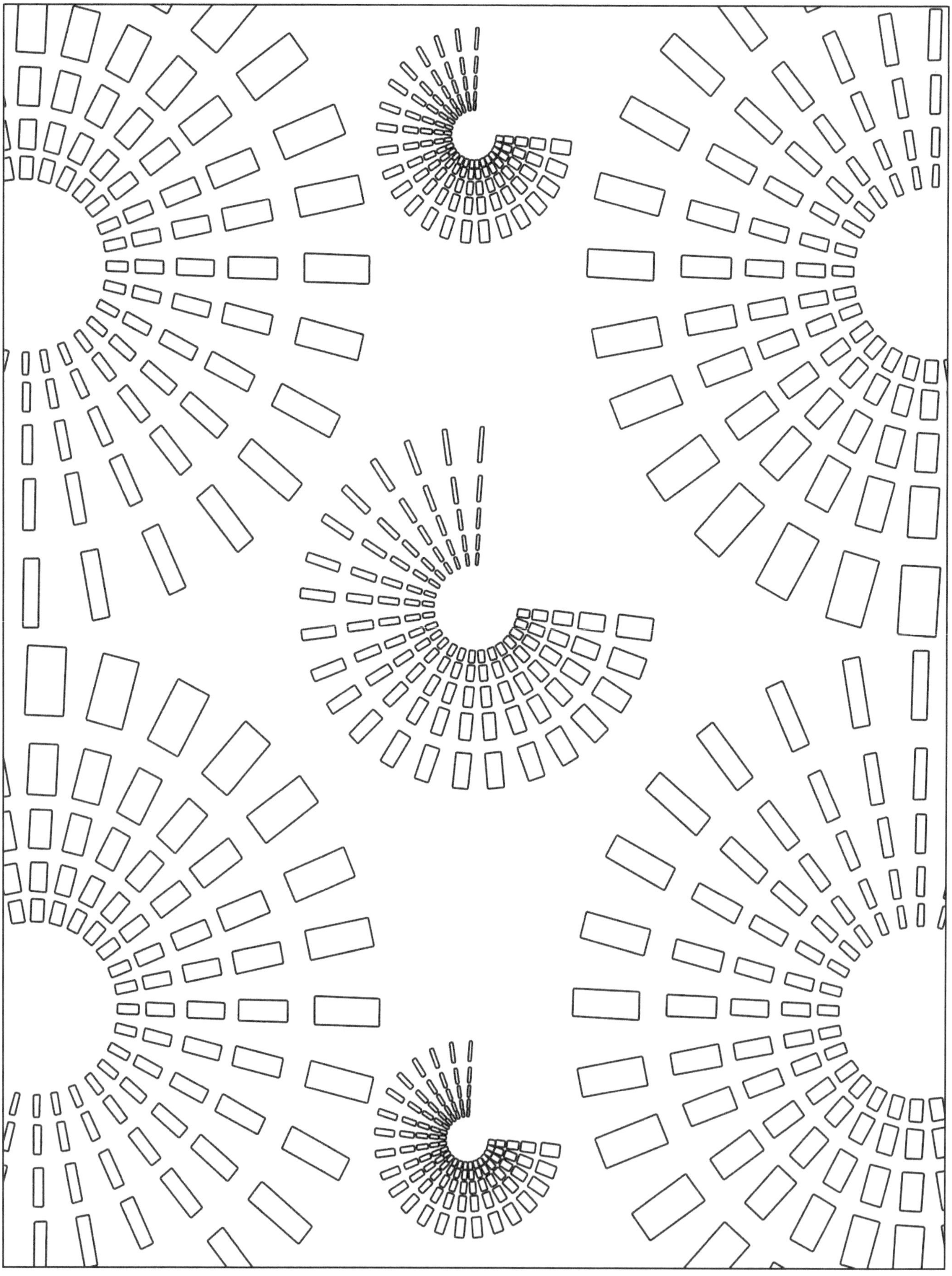

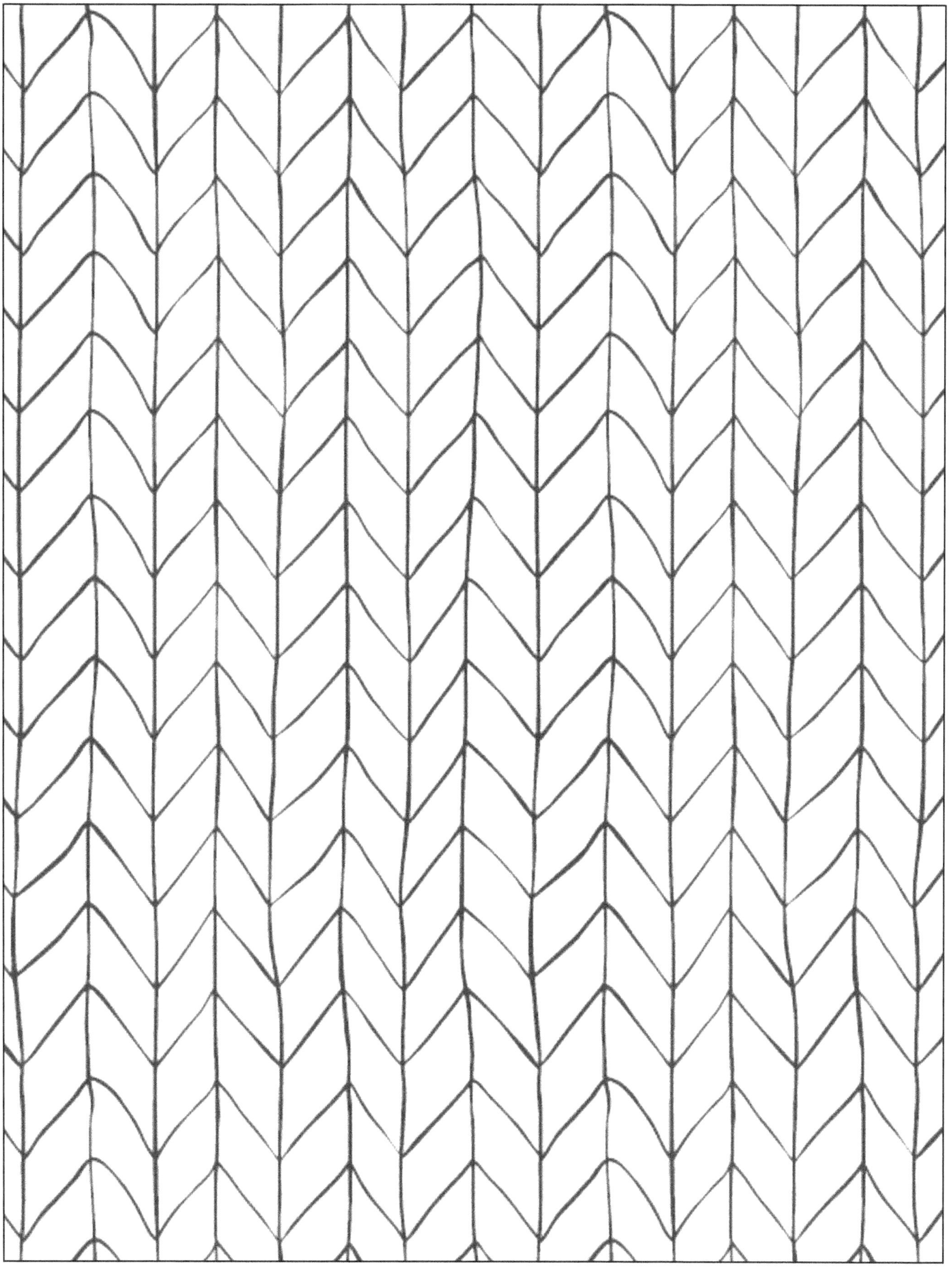

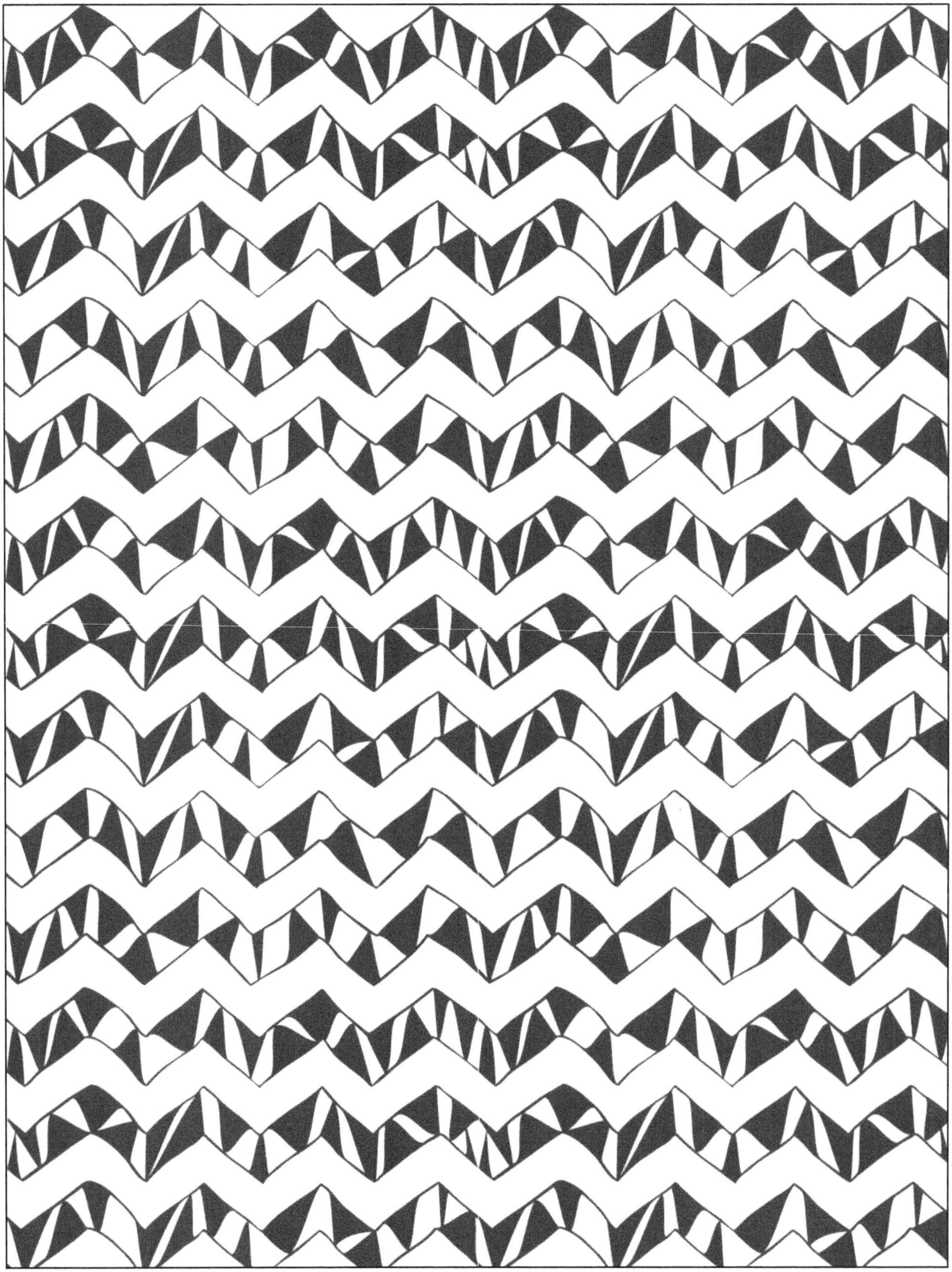

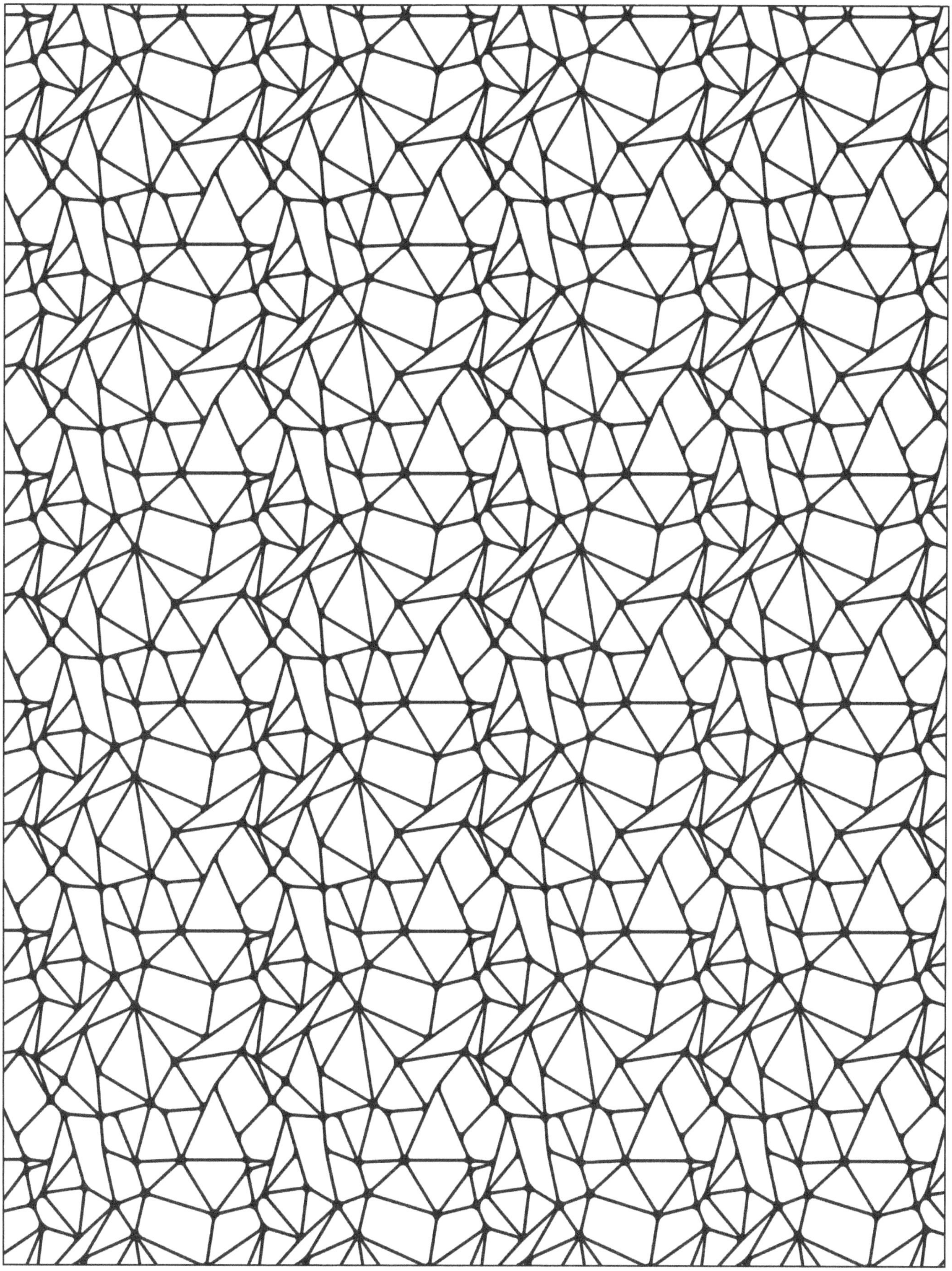

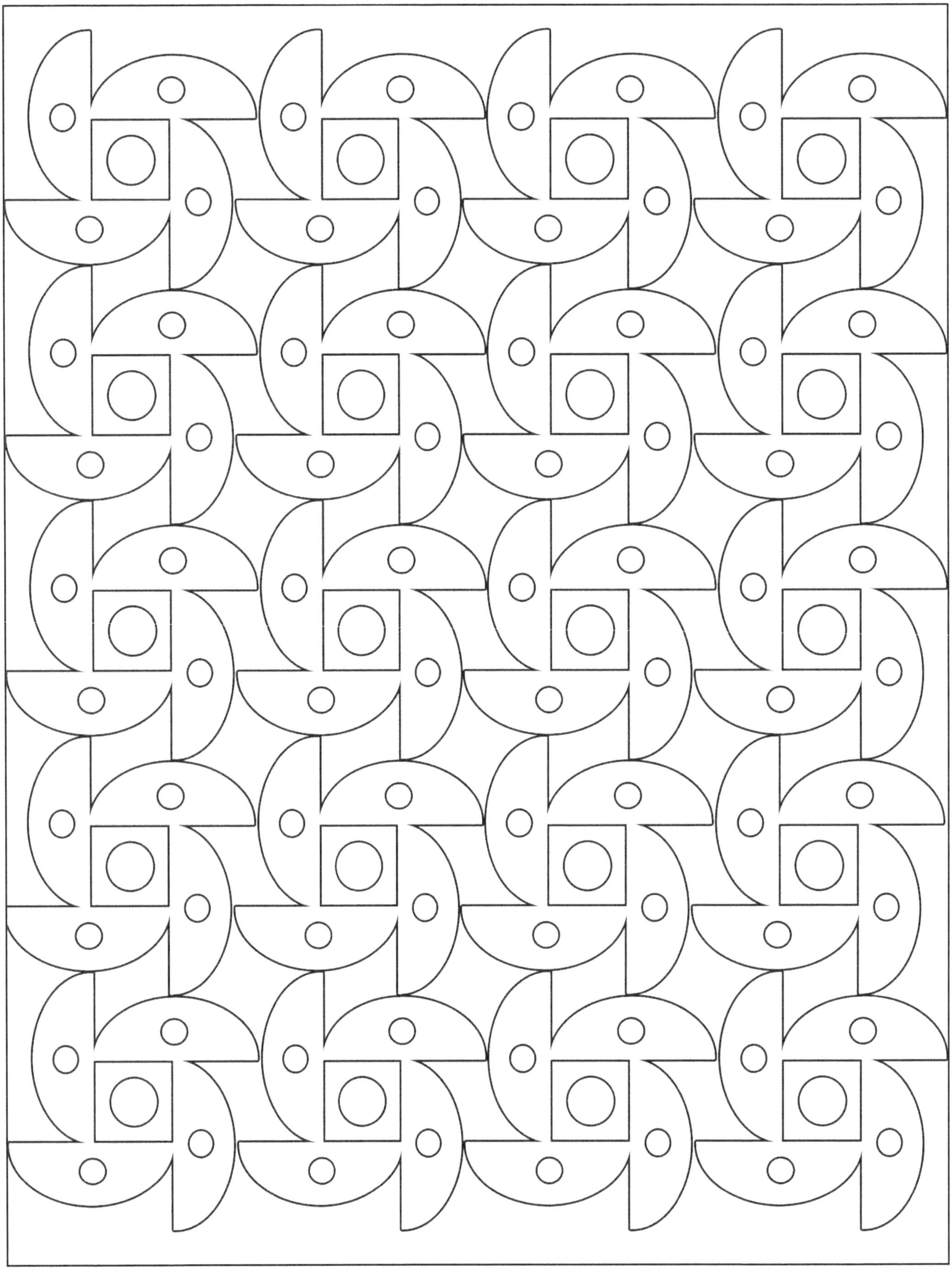

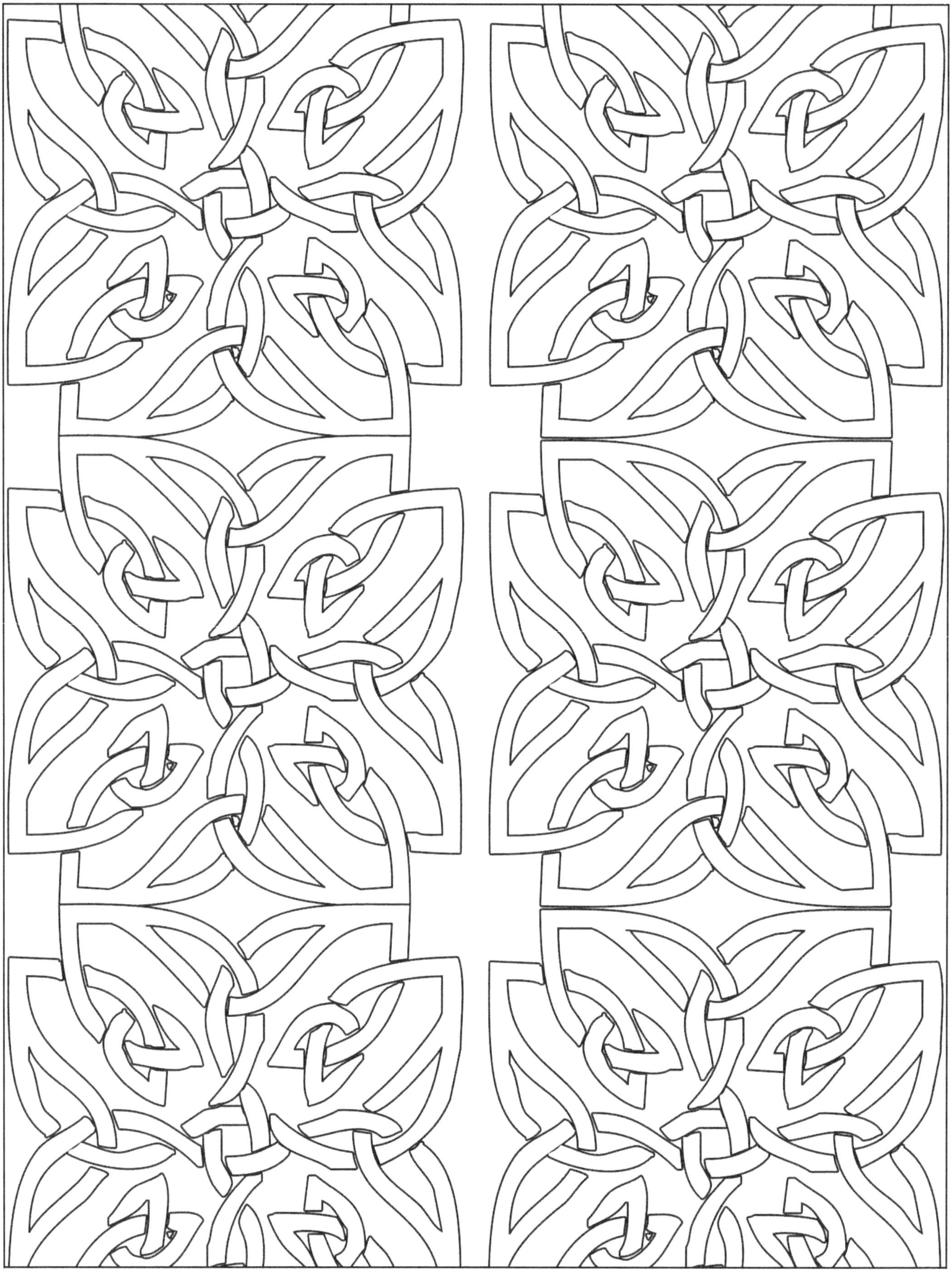

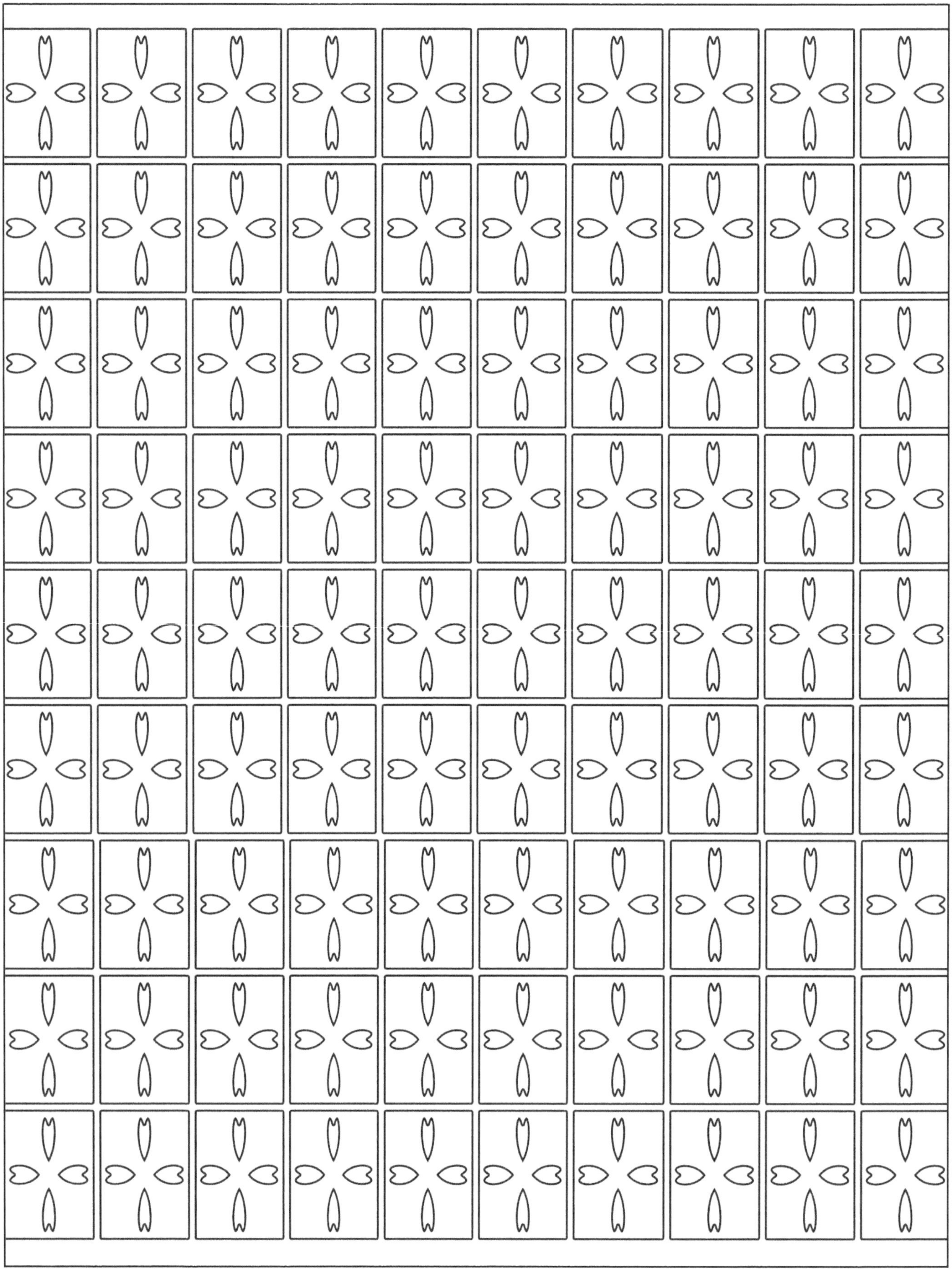

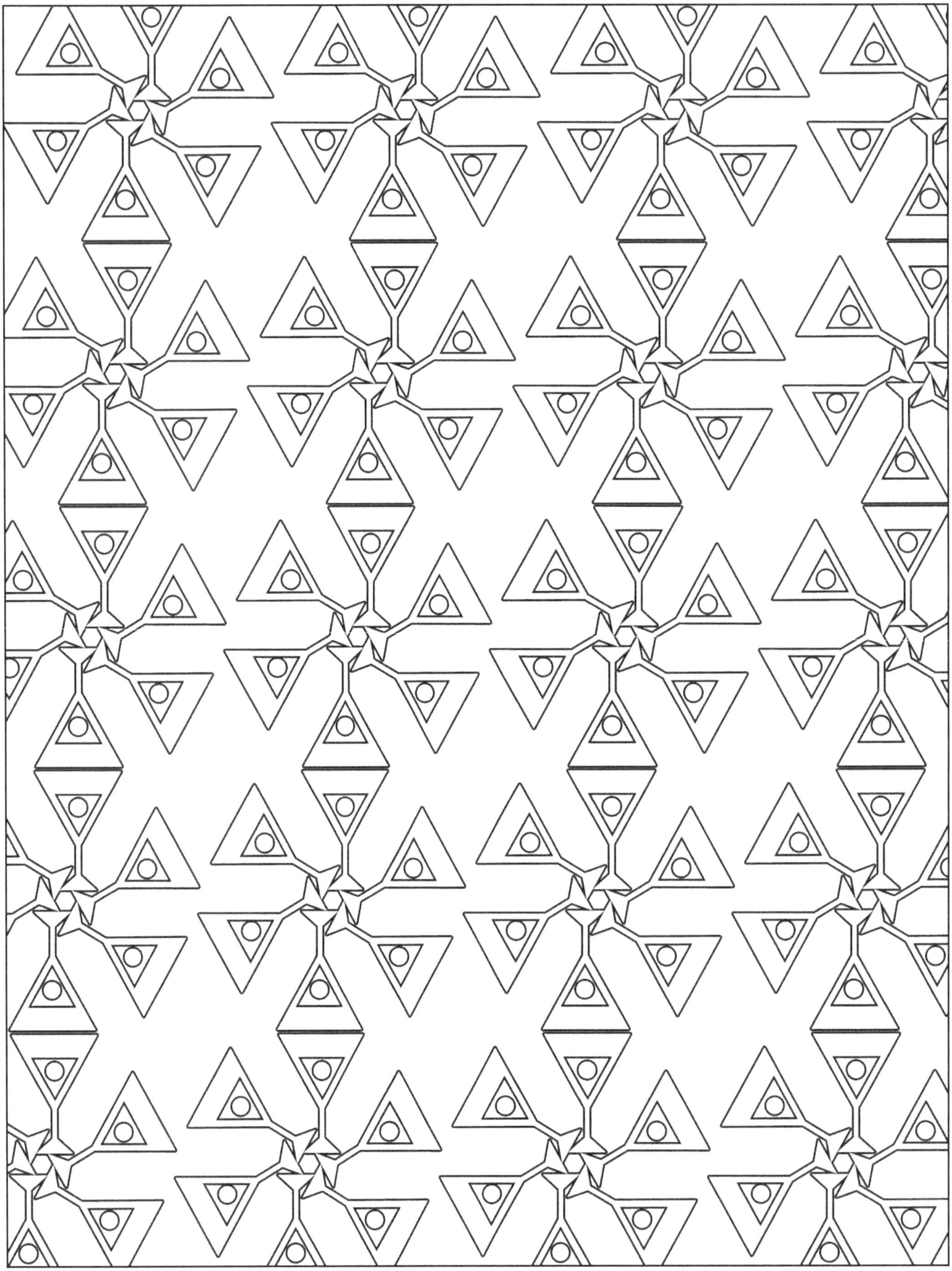

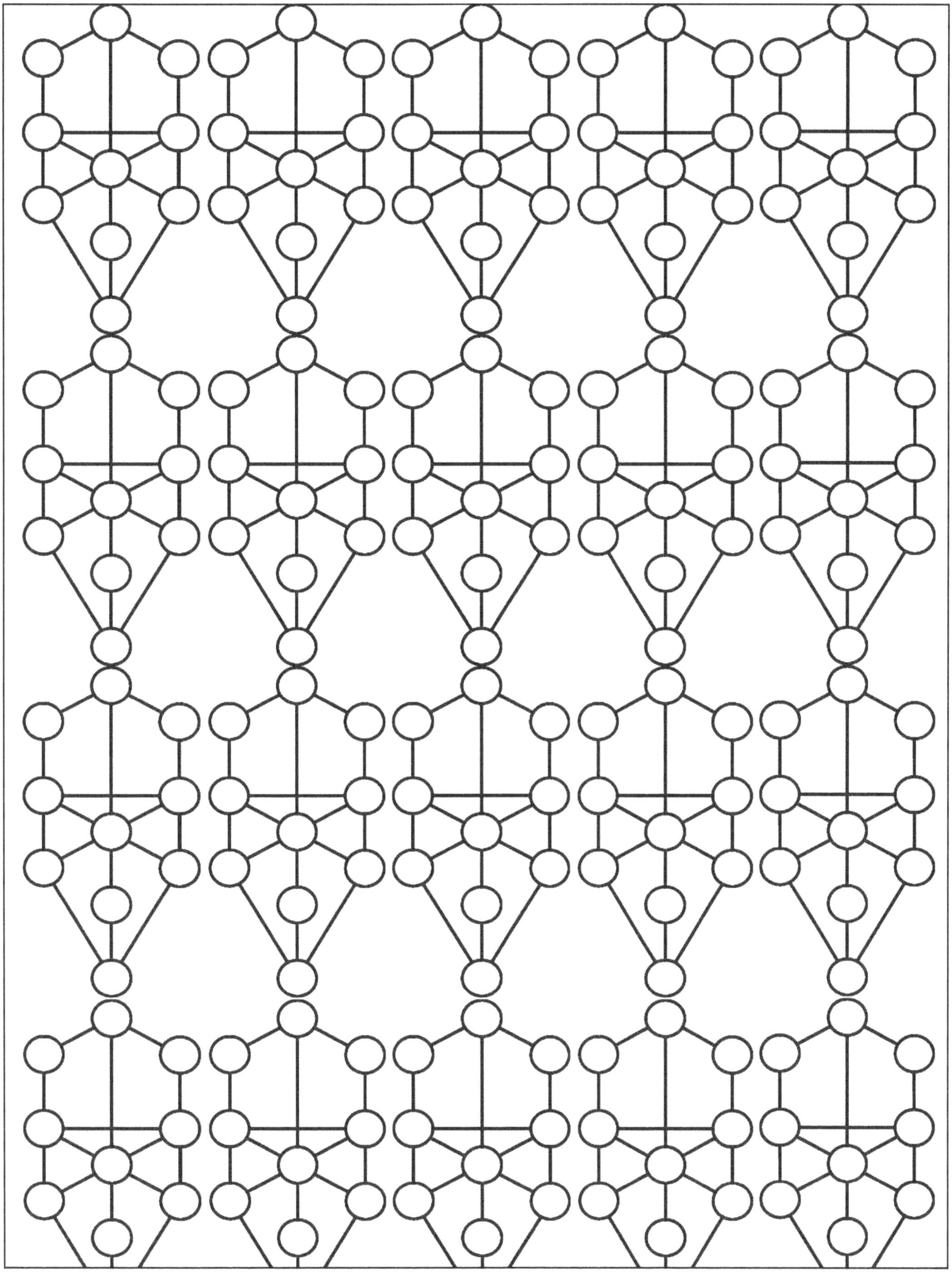

www.ingramcontent.com/pod-product-compliance
Lightning Source LLC
Chambersburg PA
CBHW080617180526
45168CB00007B/2946
* 9 7 8 1 5 1 1 8 9 3 1 6 9 *